Dying to Live

Dying to Live

A STORY OF
U.S. IMMIGRATION
IN AN AGE OF
GLOBAL APARTHEID

JOSEPH NEVINS
Photographs by Mizue Aizeki

Open Media/City Lights Books
San Francisco

The Open Media Series is edited by Greg Ruggiero and archived by The Tamiment Library, New York University

Library of Congress Cataloging-in-Publication Data
Nevins, Joseph.
 Dying to live: a story of U.S. immigration in an age of global apartheid / text by Joseph Nevins ; photos by Mizue Aizeki.
     p. cm.
 ISBN-13: 978-0-87286-486-3
 ISBN-10: 0-87286-486-3
  1. Human smuggling—Mexican-American Border Region. 2. Immigrants—Mexican-American Border Region—Death. 3. Illegal aliens—Crimes against—Mexican-American Border Region. 4. Mexico—Emigration and immigration—Social aspects. 5. United States—Emigration and immigration—Social aspects. 6. Mexican-American Border Region—Social conditions. I. Aizeki, Mizue. II. Title.
 JV6475.N47 2008
 364.1'3—dc22
 2007027987

City Lights Books are published at the City Lights Bookstore,
261 Columbus Avenue, San Francisco, CA 94133.

Dedicated to Julio César Gallegos, Don Florentino Gallegos, and José Luis Arellano, and their loved ones who survive them—and to all migrants, wherever they may find themselves, in this world and beyond.

CONTENTS

ACKNOWLEDGMENTS

A work such as this is always a collective effort in the sense that the information, analysis, and images within are the outgrowth of many conversations and the exchange of ideas, experiences, and feelings with countless individuals over many years. At the same time, such an endeavor, given the time commitment involved and the resources needed to carry it out, requires myriad forms of help from friends and colleagues.

In that regard, we thank the many people who provided invaluable support, guidance, or inspiration at different stages of this project, without whom in a collective sense we would have never completed this work. They include (and are not limited to): Shizuko Aizeki; Mona Ali; Roxane Auer; Kirti Baranwal; Alex and Anne Caputo-Pearl; Guadalupe Castillo; Margo Cowan; Garry Davis; Timothy Dunn; Mark Ellis; Isabel Garcia; Ruthie Gilmore; Gerry Hale; Scott Handleman; David Hernandez; Monica Hernandez; Roberto Hernandez; Kirsten Isaacson; Julia Ishimaru; Tore Kapstad; Scott Kerr; Scott Kessler; Yuki Kidokoro; Kim Komenich; Max Leeming; Serge Levy; Rick Miller; Enrique Morones; Richard Nevins; Nicté Ordoñez; José Palafox; Nancy Peluso; Laura Pulido, Eugene Richards; Ted Robertson; Kat Rodriguez; Raquel Rubio-Goldsmith; Kevin Rudiger; David Runsten; Dereka Rushbrook; Mark Salzer; Elizabeth Sammons; Fred Seavey; Aarti Shahani, Subhash Kateel and the members of Families for Freedom; Claudia Smith; Sam Speers; Michelle Vignes; Michael

Walsh; Michael Watts; Layla Welborn; and Ray Ybarra. At the same time, we extend our appreciation to the following organizations in southern Arizona and countless individuals associated with them for helping and teaching us in so many ways, and for their ongoing work: Derechos Humanos, No More Deaths, the Samaritan Patrols, Humane Borders, and Casa Maria/The Catholic Worker.

A number of individuals generously took the time to engage the project and provide critical feedback on different aspects of it. For that, we express our deep appreciation to David Bacon, Frank Bardacke (and Pam Sexton for connecting us to him), Lian Hurst Mann and Eric Mann and the Labor/Community Strategy Center, Amitava Kumar, and Joe Rodriguez. Lydia Savage and Tyrone Simpson both read the entire manuscript and gave invaluable feedback, generously taking time out of their busy lives and sharing their critical insights. Special thanks goes to Michael Velarde at Vassar College; he pored over the manuscript multiple times and provided all sorts of constructive criticisms and helpful ideas, while also assisting with research and production matters. Thanks as well to Elizabeth Graves for assistance with research.

In addition, we express our appreciation to people who generously shared their time in providing specific pieces of information, analysis, or materials. Among them are Raúl Delgado-Wise, Joe Heyman, Miguel Moctezuma Longoria, Rick Macken, Bruce Parks, Eric Peters, and Ken Verdoia.

Thanks to Adam Harju and the *Imperial Valley Press* for allowing us to include one of his photos in the book. Thanks as well to Zoltán Grossman for sharing his cartographic skills and making the maps we use.

During our visits to Juchipila, Zacatecas, many people generously welcomed us, and provided information and analysis. Among those we would like to thank are Doña "Chole" (Soledad) and family, the late Don Florentino Gallegos, Don Salvador Esparza, Hugo Horacio Hernandez Jauregui, Martín Lopez, and Profesor Raúl López

Robles. We extend a very special thanks to (the late) José Luis Arellano and Elvia Bañuelos Lara, as well as to their extended families, for their warm hospitality and friendship.

The book would not have been possible without Jackie Murillo's support and willingness to open her home and heart to us from the beginning of the project. We are profoundly grateful to her and the members of the extended Murillo and Gallegos families, especially Jesús and Vicky Gallegos, "Tino" Gallegos, Alejandra and Jorge Rodríguez, Doña Maria Rodríguez, and Jackie and Julio's sons, Andrew and Julio Jr.

Anthony Arnove, our agent, was enthusiastic about the book from its earliest stages. We are most grateful to him for his selfless work on behalf of this endeavor, for his solidarity, and for helping us to find an appropriate publisher.

It has been a great pleasure to work with Greg Ruggiero, our editor at City Lights Books. We thank him for his patience, support, and excellent work in bringing the book to fruition. Thanks also to Stacey Lewis for her enthusiasm for, and active commitment to, promoting the book, to Stewart Cauley for designing the cover, and to Gambrinus for designing the text.

We are also very appreciative for the financial assistance from Vassar College—in the form of two faculty research grants—which were of great help in paying for research trips to Arizona, California, and Juchipila, Zacatecas.

Finally, we thank our parents—Hiroko and Shin Aizeki, and Carol Nevins—for their support throughout this project, and for a list of things so long we do not even dare to start it, and our daughters, Amina and Sayako, for the joy, laughter, love, and richness they have brought to our lives.

—Mizue Aizeki and Joseph Nevins
Poughkeepsie, New York

AUTHOR'S NOTE ON LANGUAGE

In writing this book, I've struggled with what to call people, how to categorize them. Terms such as "illegal immigrant," for example, effectively criminalize individuals for entering or residing in a country without the sanction of the national government, while privileging the perspective of the state. In the contemporary political climate, "illegal" has become for many a code word for ethno-racial hatred toward unwanted migrants. For such reasons, whenever I use the term "illegal" in relation to migrants or immigration, I put it in quotation marks. More typically, I use terms such as "unauthorized."

Regarding ethno-racial distinctions, I sometimes use the term "nonwhite." While it is far from ideal to utilize a term to describe people by what they are *not*, it sometimes serves as an effective shorthand given the diverse ethno-racial composition of particular areas at specific times. More important, in discussing places like Southern California in the 1880s and early 1900s, "nonwhite" is appropriate given that the primary social divide—as dictated by the region's political elites—was that between people who were deemed to be "white" and those who were not. Indeed, "white" was the effective equivalent of "American."

If, during the time period mentioned above, racial categories were clear—at least rhetorically—those of citizenship were less so. People of Mexican descent born in the territory annexed by the

United States through its war with Mexico, for instance, were—by the terms of the treaty that ended the conflict in 1848—U.S. citizens. Nonetheless, local, state, and federal officials rarely accorded them the full rights and privileges of such citizenship in the many decades that followed. Instead, they often perceived and treated all people of Mexican descent—regardless of citizenship status—as, at best, second-class inhabitants of what had become the United States. As such, the term "Mexican" was typically applied to the entire Mexican-origin population without any distinction made between those who were U.S. citizens and those who were not. Thus, in much of the literature I draw upon for this book, the citizenship status of the specific people of Mexican ancestry in question is often not clear. (This is also true for other ethno-racial groups such as people of Japanese ancestry.) Although the process of distinguishing between Mexican nationals and U.S. citizens of Mexican descent was a gradual one, World War II and its aftermath seem to be a time of marked change. As such, I use the term "Mexican" for all people of Mexican descent until the World War II era, while employing "Mexican-American" when appropriate in discussing the post-World War II period.

Despite having made these choices, I hardly feel comfortable with them. Philosopher Ludwig Wittgenstein's observation that "words are deeds" highlights why it is so difficult to figure out the proper terms to categorize groups of people. As Wittgenstein suggests, words embody our ways of life. To the extent that they are meaningful, they flow from, and help produce our worldviews and everyday practices. But given the complex and ever-changing categories of identity and the larger social relations of which they are part, our words are significantly limited in terms of what they can illuminate. At the same time, to the extent that one wants to challenge language that contributes to a devaluing and marginalization of human beings simply on account of their ancestry, geographic origin, or on what side of an international divide they were born, the effort to identify appropriate terms is part of a larger struggle—one to create a different, more just world.

Imperial County, California, U.S.A. March 2001. Trained in tracking (a technique used by hunters), a Border Patrol agent estimated that migrants had made these footprints twelve hours prior.

ONE **THE BODIES**

IT WAS A LITTLE AFTER 9:00 A.M. on August 13, 1998, when Ralph Smith, the deputy coroner for California's Imperial County, received the phone call. About two hours earlier, a ranch foreman passing through a United States Border Patrol checkpoint on State Route 86 had informed agents that there was a group of people in trouble in the desert about six miles south of nearby State Route 78.[1]

Using an airplane and some agents on the ground, the Border Patrol located the group of seven individuals—six men and one young woman—huddled together under a clump of salt cedar trees about twenty-five miles north of the U.S.-Mexico boundary.[2] They were no longer in distress, however. They were dead. The bodies had been there for at least a few weeks, and possibly for six to seven. Some of the deceased were only wearing their underwear, and there were no water containers located near the corpses. But there was no indication that any of them had suffered foul play. Photos showed bodies that were, in parts, pitch black—signs of putrefaction or mummification, ones that looked like they had been charred.[3]

One of the dead was Julio César Gallegos, father of a 2-year-old boy, Julio Jr., whose photo the authorities found in his clutched hand. Gallegos lived in East Los Angeles with his son and his wife, Jackie, eight months pregnant at the time that his body was discovered. He worked for the minimum wage ($5.15 per hour) in the nearby city of Vernon at a Chinese frozen-food factory. The 23-year-old was on his way home from a stay in Mexico, where he was visiting his elderly father.

Border Patrol officials guessed that the seven had originally been part of a group of twenty-two migrants who had crossed into California without authorization from Mexico, and had arrived in the area by automobile and were waiting for someone else to pick them up; they also determined that the group's members were all headed to Los Angeles and New York.[4] Among the dead were Julio César Gallegos's 18-year-old niece, Irma Estrada Gutierrez, and Fernando Salguero Lachino, a 48-year-old father of six children—none of them older than twelve.

According to Smith's report, Gallegos's body, like the rest, was mummified, and so severely decomposed that his eyes were destroyed. He was clad in a pair of blue jeans, and had a broken watch on his left wrist. He also was carrying a black wallet, the contents of which included a California identification card, which noted a date of birth of September 14, 1974.

It would reach 108 degrees at the height of the day in El Centro, where Smith's office and the local Border Patrol headquarters are located. On the desert floor where Gallegos lay, it was considerably hotter. By 11:00 a.m., as the coroner's office was collecting the bodies, it was already 120 degrees.

—◊—

Entering the United States from Mexico without U.S. government authorization has long been potentially fatal. As early as the late 1800s, a number of unauthorized Chinese immigrants died in the desert while trying to circumvent boundary policing resulting from the Chinese Exclusion Act of 1882.[5] During the 1980s and the early 1990s, many deaths occurred on an annual basis, the annual totals reaching a high point in 1988 and gradually diminishing through the early 1990s. But with the dramatic buildup of the boundary enforcement infrastructure initiated during the early years of the Clinton administration, the number of crossing-related fatalities has steadily grown, reaching historic highs, averaging more than 350 documented deaths per year between 1995 and 2006, and doubling in terms of annual average between 1999 and 2005.[6]

In both relative and absolute terms, the number of migrant deaths brought about by environmental factors, especially extreme heat, has also increased since the mid-1990s. Along the U.S.-Mexico boundary, heat exposure today appears to be by far the most common cause of death. At the same time, greater numbers of fatalities are taking

Imperial County, California, U.S.A. August 1998. Recovery of Julio's body.
PHOTO BY ADAM HARJU FOR THE *IMPERIAL VALLEY PRESS.*

place in fairly remote areas as migrants cross in increasingly isolated zones to avoid detection by the ever-larger enforcement web throughout the border region. Because of that, and because agencies such as the Border Patrol have used extremely narrow criteria over the years for counting fatalities of unauthorized crossers, the true death toll is certainly higher than the numbers based on actually recovered bodies and official counts.[7]

The grisly deaths of Julio César Gallegos and his compatriots in 1998 reflected the shifting geography of migrant fatalities and the increasing importance of environmental factors as the immediate causes of such tragedies. The discovery of their bodies raised the number of migrant corpses found in California's Imperial Valley that year to a minimum of fifty-four—the highest on record for that area at the time. Hyperthermia—or excessive body temperature—and a lack of food and water brought about their demise, according to the Imperial County coroner's office.

Hyperthermia passes through six stages, the first two being heat stress and heat fatigue. Heat syncope, the next one, results in a fever, and, simultaneously, colder skin. The afflicted's face begins to pale and she or he becomes somewhat dizzy. Heat cramps follow and lead to tightening and aching muscles, ones so painful that it can lead one to double over in pain. Heat exhaustion results in greatly heightened fever, bad headaches, nausea, and vomiting; the victim's skin is cold, shivering might occur, and fainting or cardiac arrest might result. Heat stroke, the final stage, causes one's body to become so hot that migrants often strip off their clothes to free themselves of extreme discomfort; it leads to the body's organs and muscles essentially collapsing, resulting in death in many cases. As one passes through these stages, a person becomes increasingly disoriented, undermining one's ability to take remedial action.[8]

The deaths of Julio César Gallegos and those he was traveling with generated a good deal of coverage in the news media in southern California. Indeed, the fatalities constituted the largest group of migrant corpses ever discovered in the state's border region. That Julio was trying to return to his family and home in Los Angeles and that his wife was a U.S. citizen led the media to privilege his story over those of the others who perished alongside him. And as had become routine since the mid-1990s in such high-profile cases, the deaths elicited official expressions of sorrow as well as outrage directed at professional smugglers, commonly known as *coyotes*, who federal officials blamed (and still do) for leading unauthorized migrants into deadly environments. The U.S. Immigration and Naturalization Service (INS) Western Regional director Johnny Williams characterized the migrants as "innocents" while voicing disdain for the people who had led the group into the treacherous terrain. "It's a terrible death, an excruciating death, and one nobody should have to endure," he said.[9]

The day after the discovery of the bodies, Williams announced a $5,000 reward for information leading to "the arrest and indictment of any alien smuggler responsible for the deaths." "Alien smugglers," he stated, "present one of the greatest dangers facing illegal border crossers and must be brought to justice."[10] The announcement marked the first time the INS had offered any such reward. Among other things, the reward reflected the federal government's frustration with the continuing fatalities and its need to appear to be doing something to remedy the growing death toll.

The INS's framing of the problem resonated with the larger public—at least as reflected by editorials in the mainstream media within California. The *Imperial Valley Press*, while issuing blame for the deaths to parties on both sides of the boundary, opined that "Mexican

Boyle Heights, California, U.S.A. May 2001. Julio's belongings returned in this bag by the Imperial County Coroner to Jackie.

"On Monday, his body arrived at the funeral home. But they wouldn't let us see it; it was too decomposed. Even his stuff smelled—that's why I put in mothballs. When I spoke to the INS agent, he told me that they found Julio with the baby picture in his hands."—Jackie

---

and U.S. authorities must hunt down the smugglers of human cargo and make them pay appropriate prices. If someone dies because of their crimes," the paper continued, "then the appropriate price for the 'coyote' would be a murder conviction."[11] Three days later, the *San Diego Union-Tribune* similarly pointed the finger at "ruthless and inhuman smugglers" who "take people into the remote desert and abandon them." The editorial argued for increased penalties for smugglers and called upon the U.S. and Mexican governments to "declare war on immigrant smuggling." And like the *Imperial Valley Press*, the San Diego newspaper recommended a charge of murder when "an immigrant dies of heat exposure in a smuggler's charge, or after being abandoned."[12] On the same day, the *Los Angeles Times* characterized the smugglers as people who "too often do not care whether their clients live or die" and editorialized in favor of stiffer penalties for smugglers, including life imprisonment and even the death penalty.[13] The *Times* editorial staff issued this call despite a small item in the paper's pages the previous day that reported that authorities had determined that two of the bodies found in the desert along with that of Julio César Gallegos were those of smugglers leading the group.[14]

—◦◦◦—

How and why Julio César Gallegos's body ended up on the scorched desert terrain of southern California is the outgrowth of many factors, contingent and structural, incidental and historical. One of the key factors is geography, but not geography as commonly thought of as a relatively static physical landscape or points in global space. Space, like time, is dynamic and ever-changing. While shaped to a significant degree by physical forces, geographic space is largely a social creation in terms of what is contained within it, how it is divided up and bounded, and how it is perceived and lived. It is thus a product of power relations and all the conflict—as well as cooperation—that they entail.

In seeking to explain the death—and life—of Julio César Gallegos, it is this type of geography that this book privileges. There are myriad ways in which to tell his story and those of the thousands of other migrants who have perished in the U.S.-Mexico borderlands since the mid-1990s. However, this book does so through a focus on places—the locations in which people live their lives, to which they attach meanings, which help define who they are, and thus shape to

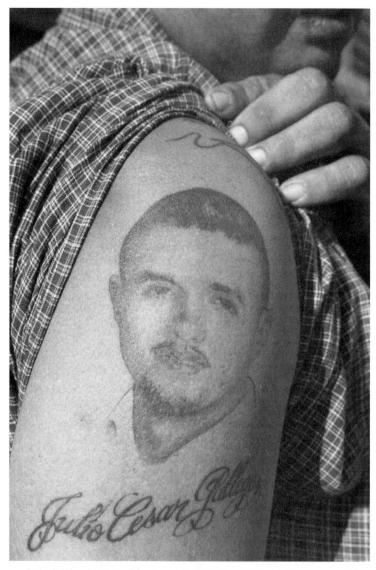

Tijuana, Baja California Norte, Mexico. July 2002. Tino, Julio's brother, at memorial service at border wall.

a large degree where they can and cannot go, reside, and work.[15]

Just as places, like any social construct, are dynamic, so, too, are the boundaries that define them. And while bounded, no place exists in isolation. It is connected and shaped by other places, and by the individuals, collectivities, and institutions associated with them. As such, a place's boundaries, just as its contents, are ever-changing. In this regard, one must appreciate how these places have come about, the power relations and associated inequalities that they embody, the vibrant connections and divisions that bring places together and, often simultaneously, drive them apart.[16] In the case of Julio César Gallegos, it was the intersection of a particular set of such connections and divisions that brought him during the summer of 1998 to southern California's Imperial Valley, one of the places that make up the geographical web that shaped his life and death.

**Colorado Desert,
Imperial Valley,
California, U.S.A.
March 2001.**
The view northward.

TWO THE DESERT

CALIFORNIA'S IMPERIAL VALLEY IS A DESERT, as well as a testimony to both the power of humans to shape the world to their needs and the limits of such power. Although rainfall rarely occurs in the area, averaging about three inches per year and dropping to an almost totally arid half inch in some years, the Imperial Valley has lush fields thanks to large-scale irrigation and is home to some of the biggest and most lucrative agribusinesses in the United States. Yet, at the same time, it is one of the lowest-income-per-capita areas in California; the region's population has a poverty rate—almost 20 percent—about twice that of the state and more than 50 percent higher than that of the country as a whole.[1]

It was this combination of desolation and development that led Julio César Gallegos and the other members of his group to try to traverse the Imperial Valley. Its relative isolation and low socioeconomic standing, and the fact that fewer unauthorized migrants crossed the boundary there than in more urbanized sections on the U.S. side of the line, resulted in it receiving far less attention in terms of boundary enforcement resources than its heavily populated and wealthy California cousin, the San Diego area, in the 1990s. That, combined with the expansive rural area surrounding the Valley's small urban concentrations like Calexico and El Centro, made it a far easier place to cross the line clandestinely—and simultaneously a more dangerous one given the distance and harsh terrain one must cover before arriving at a destination of choice. Meanwhile, its level of development resulted in the presence of infrastructure that made it possible to access more populated areas such as Los Angeles.

On a more sociological level, the Imperial Valley embodies the divisions of race, class, and nation that have long allowed some to enjoy the area's rich fruits and that have effectively marginalized or barred others from doing so. Divides between growers and farmworkers, whites and nonwhites, and "Americans" and "Mexicans"—among others—have been central to the making of the Imperial Valley since its establishment as a political-economic entity. Such divisions have also long been at the heart of U.S.-Mexico relations. In that regard, the Imperial Valley's effective rejection of Julio César Gallegos—while an extreme example of the outcome of such social classifications—is not exceptional. Race, nation, and class and their attendant inequalities—ones that have profound implications for how people live and die—have come together in the Imperial Valley since its very establishment, and in the making and unmaking of its ties to, and separation from, Mexico and beyond.

———∿∿∿———

Only a century before the discovery of the 23-year-old's body, the Imperial Valley did not exist as a political-economic entity. Calexico, California, and its twin city across the boundary, Mexicali, had not yet been founded. It was at the turn of the twentieth century that the two border towns saw their births—both beginning about 1900 as clusters of tents for laborers and engineers working for the developers who gave the two settlements their binational, hybrid names and christened the valley "Imperial,"[2] a label ironically suggestive of how the United States came to control the area.

The Valley is part of a below-sea-level basin surrounded by mountains except in the southeast portion where there are sand dunes and hills and to the east where the Yuma and Sonoran deserts are found. From northwest to southeast, it is about a hundred miles long and thirty-five miles wide. The Coachella Valley of California comprises its narrow northern end, while the Mexicali Valley of Mexico makes up its southern one. In between the two is the Imperial Valley.

Prior to the twentieth century, settlement and economic activity in the desiccated area was limited to indigenous groups such as the

Sonoyta, Sonora, Mexico. July 2006. Looking into Organ Pipe Cactus National Monument, Arizona, U.S.A.

Yuma, Cocopa, and Kamia who were attracted to the valley's rich alluvial soils transported and dropped by the seasonal floodwaters of the Colorado River. It was along these areas that the indigenous population concentrated, the most numerous being the Cocopa, who cultivated maize, beans, and pumpkins, with a population of about 22,000 at the time of European contact. The size of the indigenous population remained stable through the mid-1800s, but began declining rapidly thereafter in the face of increased contact and the onslaught of European diseases, displacement, and violence. Thus, by the beginning of the twentieth century, only a few hundred indigenous inhabitants remained, and for the most part, they ended up working for white settlers.[3]

Anglos—a term used in the U.S. Southwest to characterize Americans of European descent (other than those of Hispanic or Latino ancestry)—began coveting the area as early as the mid-1800s when fortune seekers heading to California's goldfields passed through the region, which was then known as the Colorado Desert or the Salton Sink. William Blake, a geologist, while accompanying a federal government team exploring a railroad route to the Pacific in 1853, was the first to establish on the basis of modern science the fertility of the area's soils. Blake, with the help of Cahuilla Indians indigenous to the area, ascertained that the valley floor was actually an ancient, below-sea-level lake bed, one covered with highly rich silt deposited by the flooding of the Colorado River. Cahuilla informed Blake that their ancestors had lived in the canyons above what was once the body of water that covered the area and where they came to catch fish, ducks, and other animals. They also showed the geologist their crops of corn, barley, and various vegetables, as well as their use of irrigation techniques. On the basis of what he learned and witnessed, Blake likened the river to the Nile, expressing the view that it was "probable that the greater part of the desert could be made to yield crops of almost any kind" provided that "a supply of water could be obtained for irrigation."[4]

Such words were indicative of a dramatic shift in how most Americans perceived the desert. At the time of the U.S. annexation of the Southwest in 1848, the dominant view of the desert in the United States was that of a harsh, foreboding zone, as one of little value, and primarily as an area of passage that connected California to the rest of the country east of the arid stretch. This view began to change in the late 1850s with the discovery of minerals. As such, the desert was increasingly seen as a place for extraction and prospectors, but still having little aesthetic worth. And about the turn of the twentieth century, others began to regard the desert as a site to master—through large-scale irrigation and other environment-transforming tools. In this view, the desert would be made to retreat and rendered suitable for modern agriculture and for civilization more broadly.[5] While many countered such a worldview (and still do) and instead saw the desert as an ecologically rich and intrinsically beautiful area worthy of preservation, the notion of it as a site to be conquered and transformed became and remains dominant in political-economic terms, its roots located in a longstanding view that the desert is first and foremost something to be overcome.

And overcoming the desert was exactly what Blake was proposing in the Imperial Valley. An entrepreneurial engineer by the name of Charles Rockwood was a key figure in realizing Blake's vision. In 1896, Rockwood formed the California Development Company to bring the waters of the Colorado River to the Salton Sink. It took Rockwood about four years to secure sufficient funding—from George Chaffey, a very successful civil engineer and irrigation expert from southern California. Chaffey, in signing a contract that enjoined him to build the desired canal system, became the president and chief engineer of the company.

The California Development Company dug a canal from the Colorado River. The canal's route took it south into Mexico along the boundary for a few miles into the dry channel of the Alamo River and then back up north. On May 14, 1901, a network of feeder canals began irrigating hundreds of farms in the Imperial Valley, leading to an intensification of a land rush that had already begun.[6]

As the California Development Company was only in the business of selling water, Chaffey formed another company, the Imperial Land Company, to attract settlers, build towns, and construct productive farms. In part by imposing an attractive name—it was feared that names like Salton Sink and Colorado Desert might scare away would-be colonists and investors—the newly baptized Imperial Valley soon saw the arrival of settlers, the first of whom came in 1901.[7] It also quickly attracted many small investors—especially from New England, but from all over the eastern part of the United States.

By 1902, there were 400 miles of irrigation canals and dug ditches, sufficient water for at least 100,000 acres of irrigable land. In addition, the towns of Calexico and Imperial had been laid out. By the end of the year, there were 2,000 settlers. A year later there were 7,000. By 1909, the population of the Imperial Valley had grown to 15,000 and there were 160,000 acres of land under irrigation.[8] Where before there had been open desert, there were soon towns such as Holtville, El Centro, Brawley, Heber, and Westmorland. The newly arrived settlers produced a large variety of crops—most of them water-intensive—including table grapes, grapefruit, apricots, cotton, yams, wheat, asparagus, and potatoes. Most lucrative were melons, especially cantaloupes.[9]

A novel published in 1911, *The Winning of Barbara Worth*, enshrined and celebrated these developments, and helped publicize them throughout the United States. The best-selling novel (its first printing was 175,000 copies) tells the story of a four-year-old girl found in the forbidding desert near the corpse of her mother by a small group of hardy men. The mother had given her daughter her last drops of water and, as a result, had died of thirst. One of the men, a wealthy financier named Jefferson Worth, adopts the orphan. Over the years that follow, the girl, Barbara, grows into a beautiful, young woman of strength, virtue, and independence. Her trajectory is intimately linked to the transformation of the desert—from a place of death and poverty to one of life and Progress. She embodies all that is good among the Anglo settlers: virtuous innocence, a Protestant work ethic, and a generous humility that leads her to help the area's "worthy poor." She was, wrote the author, "an angel of mercy" who gave alms to the poor and was "greatly loved" by the very same people who disliked her capitalist father.[10] Little did they know that it was he who knowingly gave Barbara the financial means to provide aid to them.

While a work of fiction, Harold Bell Wright, the book's author, states in the acknowledgment that "I must in honesty admit that this work [the development of the Imperial Valley] which in the past ten years has transformed a vast, desolate waste into a beautiful land of homes, cities, and farms, has been my inspiration." Wright, who in 1907 bought a ranch near El Centro, the Imperial Valley's major settlement, and Holtville, describes a process of civilizing the desolate area, part of a chain of progress—a worldview championed by many of the Valley's elites.[11] As Wright penned, "In the Southwest savage race succeeded savage race, until at last the slow-footed padres overtook the swift-footed Indian and the rude civilization made possible by the priests in turn ran down the priest."[12]

The latest stage in this progressive history is capitalism, presented as an inexorable force that tames the wild for the good. Wright refers to it as "Good Business—the master passion of the race." It is thus hardly surprising that the hero of the novel is a businessman, Jefferson Worth.

Worth is a man of vision. Gazing at the desert basin, under which lay "hundreds of thousands of acres equal in richness to the famous delta lands of the Nile," he foresaw

> an army of men beginning at the river and pushing out into the desert with their canals, bringing with them the life-giving water. Soon, with the coming of the water, would begin the coming of the settlers. Hummocks would be leveled, washes and arroyos filled, ditches would be made to the company canals, and in place of the thin growth of gray-green desert vegetation with the ragged patches of dun earth would come great fields of luxuriant alfalfa, billowing acres of grain, with miles upon miles of orchards, vineyards and groves. The fierce desert life would give way to the herds and flocks and the home life of the farmer. The railroad would stretch its steel strength into this new world; towns and cities would come to be where now was only solitude and desolation; and out from this world-old treasure house vast wealth would pour to enrich the peoples of the earth. The wealth of an empire lay in that land under the banker's eye, and Capital held the key.[13]

However, unlike slick East Coast businessmen who served capital, Jefferson Worth "sought to make Capital serve the race." He was a man "laboring with his brother man, sharing their hardships, sharing their returns; a man using money as a workmen uses his tools to fashion and build and develop, adding thus to the welfare of human kind."[14]

But the humanity to which Wright refers is clearly one with a steep hierarchy within—one made evident even within his novel. The author, for example, describes the population of Mexican origin with a combination of scorn and pity, writing that they live in "the adobe houses of earlier days, with tents and shacks of every description . . . scattered in careless disorder," while describing the children as "half-naked." At the same time, he exhibits a certain respect, but a patronizing one, for the dignified poverty that some Mexicans display as when Barbara visits a family, one "of the better class of industrious poor Mexicans," she has befriended and to whom she delivers tokens of charity.[15]

Mexicans, Native Americans, and "Chinamen," among others, work for Anglos in the book. Wright presents them throughout the novel, when they respectfully follow orders, as docile people of simplicity. But when they do not follow Anglo dictates, as when they do not receive the pay that is owed to them (because of circumstances the Anglo bosses cannot avoid), he depicts them as unreasonable, insufficiently patient, and quick to resort to violence. "If they were white men," one of the Anglo characters observes, "it would be different."[16] At other times, when they challenge the authority of Jefferson Worth and his Anglo sidekicks, the author characterizes Mexicans as "cholos" and "greasers."[17] Thus, there are good Mexicans—ones that do not challenge the status quo and the highly hierarchical social order—and bad ones. The same dichotomy presumably applies to non-Anglos more broadly.

———

Wright's characterizations surely resonated with many of the Anglos that began populating the area at the turn of the twentieth century. By that time, California already had a highly stratified racial pecking order, in part a legacy of both Spanish and Mexican control of the territory.[18] Native Americans were at the bottom of the ranking, a

Douglas, Arizona, U.S.A. June 2004. Apprehension of migrants by U.S. Border Patrol.

"We're fortunate enough to live in a country where there are lots of opportunities. And most of the people who we run into out here want to make that dream happen. Unfortunately, it's our job to stop that dream. That's what we do on an everyday basis."
—Border Patrol Agent Elizier Vasquez (Politzer 2007)

product of a strict racial hierarchy that informed the structure of California from the time of its incorporation into the United States. White Californians saw "Indians" as their opposite and on the bottom of humanity's ladder.[19]

Anglo California deemed Mexicans, by contrast, to be "half-civilized" and closer to European American notions of civilization than were Native peoples. This was due to what was perceived as the mixed European ancestry and the resulting linguistic and religious practices of Mexicans. In addition, the lingering political influence of the pre-U.S. conquest Mexican or *Californio* elite had a moderat-

ing effect on the most extreme forms of Anglo anti-Mexican sentiment. The position of Asian immigrants was located somewhere in
between the "half-civilized" Mexicans and the "uncivilized" indigenous population. But given what were perceived to be their highly
different cultural practices, Asians were deemed as far more uncivilized than not, and closer to Native Americans in the racial
hierarchy.[20]

It was in this ideological context that the influx of Anglos into California quickly worked to marginalize the territory's pre-1848
population. As of 1848, the non-Indian population of California was
approximately 15,000, the majority of whom were Mexican Californians who lived alongside a few thousand European Americans. But
the discovery of gold in California in 1848 changed matters rapidly.
By 1849, the Anglo population was approximately 100,000 while that
of Mexican origin was only 13,000. By 1870, the state's population
had risen to more than 500,000. Although China, Germany, England,
Ireland, and France were the most important countries of origin for
immigrants to California, native-born (Anglo) Americans were the
largest segment of California's new residents.[21]

The state's Native population—whose estimated size as of 1852
was 85,000—was the most adversely affected by the Americanization of California. The population, numbering between 300,000
and 700,000 or more in 1769 when the first Franciscan mission in
the region had been established, had already experienced a precip-
itous decline prior to the time the United States annexed the
territory. Indeed, the pre-1769 population had been substantially
larger. A combination of Spanish violence and disease—which,
according to historian David Stannard, typically went hand in
hand—took a very large toll on the population. The missionaries
and their military allies, by forcibly making Native Americans settle on their grounds, systematically overworking them and

providing woefully inadequate diets, and exposing them to diseases, turned the missions into "furnaces of death."[22] Post-conquest, a combination of diseases (the most significant factor), malnutrition and starvation, enslavement, and military and (Anglo) vigilante violence—much of it officially sanctioned—quickly led to an almost total decimation of what remained of the indigenous population. By 1860, its number had plunged to 35,000. At the end of the century, only 15,000 Native Americans survived in California, most of them, in Stannard's words, "stored safely away on remote and impoverished reservations, suffering from diseases, malnutrition, and despair."[23]

In terms of people of Mexican descent, white Californians did not ruthlessly marginalize them, but rather tried to integrate them into American society—albeit in a very much subordinated position. Initially Mexicans greatly outnumbered Anglos in post-annexation California. And unlike Native Americans, adult males of Mexican origin (ones not characterized as Indian or mestizo, but as white) had the right of suffrage. But this right was more often than not meaningless in practice as California's legislature did not define what constituted a white Mexican. As a result, localities determined racial status, and disenfranchised most of the Mexican-origin population. In addition, the rapid influx of white settlers enabled the new Anglo elite to legislate the subordination of the Mexican population, passing a number of laws in the state legislature aimed at people of Mexican descent, regardless of whether or not they were U.S. citizens. The legislature, for example, passed prohibitions against traditional Mexican cultural activities as well as an antivagrancy law—the so-called Greaser Act—which defined as vagrants "all persons who [were] commonly known as 'Greasers' or the issue of Spanish or Indian blood."[24] Economically, a combination of capitalist market forces combined with a new system of taxation that imposed levies on land, rather than on the products of the land, created great hardship for much of the Mexican landed class, contributing to widespread dispossession.[25] As a result, the Mexican population became increasingly "alienized" and proletarianized, serving to intensify the apartheid-like relationship between whites—who usually occupied positions of management and white-collar and relatively-skilled positions—and Mexicans working in the poorly paid, blue-collar, manual labor and service positions.[26]

This race-class-nation hierarchy manifested itself sharply in the Imperial Valley. Although Anglos were by far the biggest group, the area's ethnic and racial composition was heterogeneous at the beginning of the twentieth century. Japanese laborers, tenant farmers, and sharecroppers rubbed shoulders with low numbers of Asian Indians, most of whom were Punjabis and Sikhs, and a small percentage Muslims (nonetheless, they were all referred to as "Hindus" in California), and with whom they sometimes competed for jobs in the melon fields.

The workforce's diversity—especially in terms of Mexican laborers—grew as the Valley's growers first launched cotton on a massive scale in 1910. Cotton's production expanded rapidly—so much so that farmers began referring to the region as the "Egypt of America." In this context, they heavily recruited Mexicans and blacks from the U.S. South, refusing to employ Japanese, as they wanted workers who had experience with the crops. These Anglo growers were wary of the Japanese, whom they saw as tending to demand high wages and prone to organizing to defend their interests. While blacks (as well as whites from cotton-growing areas) steadily moved into the area, and Filipino laborers began arriving to participate in the harvests in 1916, their numbers were not sufficient. Mexican farmhands, many of them experienced cotton pickers, proved to be the growers' temporary salvation—even if many of the area's Anglos were unhappy with the presence of Mexicans in residential areas of towns such as El Centro and Imperial.[27]

The Valley's racial hierarchy was complicated and allowed for a certain degree of mobility and mixing. Sikhs, while small in number and frequently discriminated against, for example, often intermarried and had business relationships with whites. Many of the area's grocers were Syrian, Jewish, and Chinese. And although whites owned most of the agricultural establishments, Japanese and Sikhs owned some as well. In other cases, they leased them from Anglo absentee landlords.[28]

The number of such farms would have undoubtedly been greater had California not passed the Alien Land Law in 1913—and, more important, another law in 1920 that closed its loopholes—which prohibited the ownership and long-term lease of agricultural land to individuals ineligible for U.S. citizenship. The intended focus of the legislation was Japanese farmers, whom many Anglos saw as overly successful and a threat to their well-being. It was part of a larger effort to rid the state of the "Japanese menace" and discourage further immigration from Japan. The legislation led to many Japanese losing their land—although many got around the laws somewhat by buying land through so-called middleman arrangements (an eligible party would purchase the land for a Japanese farmer, typically for a fee), disguised tenant farming, or leasing land through companies. Nonetheless, the legislation no doubt greatly stymied the growth in the number of farms owned by non-citizen Japanese (as well as by Asian Indians who immigration authorities classified as nonwhite) in the Valley—as it did throughout the state. It also contributed to the racialization of Japanese and Asians more broadly.[29] (Racialization involves the construction of a group of people as threatening owing to supposedly essential characteristics on the basis of shared geographic origin or ancestry.)

In terms of labor, whites dominated the Valley in 1910. But as agricultural production expanded—especially in terms of cotton, cantaloupes, and lettuce—and World War I created labor shortages, Mexican labor increased significantly. Growers in the Valley and throughout Southern California began to recruit Mexican workers in the war's aftermath—a development necessitated not only by war-related shortages, but also by the 1917 Immigration Act, which intensified restrictions against East and South Asian immigration. Various loopholes and exemptions further facilitated Mexican labor migration.[30] By 1927, there were at least 20,000 Mexicans living in Imperial County—out of a total population of roughly 54,500 people, about 53 percent of whom were white. The vast majority of Mexican laborers resided in the Valley, with only a small number crossing the boundary from Mexico for seasonal employment.[31]

The number of Mexican immigrants to California tripled between 1920 and 1930. And at first, California growers were quite effusive in their praise of Mexican laborers.[32] Many explicitly saw them as superior to white workers—at least in terms of the perceived needs of agricultural interests. According to an agribusiness representative from the Imperial Valley, "Mexicans are much preferred to whites. Once fixed, they are permanent and reliable. I do not think they are good for other types of labor."[33] Moreover, in addition to their "willingness" to work for low wages, Mexican laborers were seen as highly "flexible"— to use a contemporary business term—in part because of their noncitizen status and their proximity to their homeland. As John Steinbeck wrote in 1936 about the initial attraction of Mexican workers,

> To the large grower, the Mexican labor offered more advantages than simply its cheapness. It could be treated as so much scrap when it was not needed. Any local care for the sick and crippled could be withheld; and, in addition, if it offered any

resistance to the low wage or the terrible living conditions, it could be deported to Mexico at Government expense.[34]

Yet, many still argued against the importation of Mexicans in the early twentieth century, often on the basis of the supposed threat they represented to Anglo racial hegemony. But the supporters of Mexican migrant labor had strong rebuttals to those who feared that a Mexican influx would undermine the United States. The supporters and detractors—despite their contrary policy recommendations—shared a racist underpinning for their positions. In a 1926 congressional hearing, for example, W. H. Knox of the Arizona Cotton Growers' Association offered an explanation that explicitly embraced such logic:

> Have you ever heard, in the history of the United States, or in the history of the human race, of the white race being overrun by a class of people of the mentality of the Mexicans? I never have. We took this country from Mexico. Mexico did not take it from us. To assume that there is any danger of any likelihood of the Mexican coming in here and colonizing this country and taking it away from us, to my mind, is absurd.[35]

And for those who feared the "mongrelization" of the "white race" from miscegenation, or so-called race-mixing, with Mexican immigrants, supporters of Mexican immigration advised that there was little reason for concern.[36] Harry Chandler, publisher of the *Los Angeles Times* and a large landowner in the Imperial Valley, informed Congress that Mexicans "do not intermarry like the negro with white people. They do not mingle. They keep to themselves. That is the safety of it."[37] A lobbyist for California growers explained to a congressional committee that "the Mexican likes the sunshine against an

(Top) Yuma, Arizona, U.S.A. July 2006. (Bottom) Holtsville, California, U.S.A. March 2001.
Graves of "John Does" in public cemeteries. According to Professor Wayne Cornelius of the University of California, San Diego, at least one-third of migrants who die while crossing are never identified and are buried in "potter's fields" like the ones shown above. (U.S. Commission on Civil Rights 2002)

adobe wall with a few tortillas and in the off time he drifts across the border where he may have these things."[38]

But the growers' love for Mexican laborers quickly disappeared as these workers became involved in labor unions and often participated in strikes, the Imperial Valley being a center of such. Many workers in the area did not easily resign themselves to the region's working conditions, one dictated by the seventy-four, large-scale grower-shippers who produced or financed 90 percent of the Valley's agricultural output. Like California agriculture as a whole, the Imperial Valley was marked by absentee landowners, tenant farming, widespread insecurity for laborers, and large-scale and highly concentrated land-holdings; the Times-Mirror Company (owner of the *Los Angeles Times*) and the Southern Pacific Railroad Company—which obtained much of the California Development Company's stock in 1905 in the context of a disastrous flood that ruined the company[39]—were the two largest landholders.[40] From a production perspective, however, the Valley's agriculture was highly successful, taking off after 1910. By 1950, it was number five among California's agricultural counties, and within another decade it was number two.[41] Given such scale and concentration of landholdings, one commentator in the 1930s argued that production was more industrial than agricultural in any sort of traditional sense.[42]

Working and living conditions during this time were often inhumane. One observer likened the "present servitude" of the Valley's Mexican workforce as "not very different from that imposed upon them by the conquistadors and padres."[43] The related injustices were often invisible to the Anglo population, or at least seen as the natural order of things—or perceived as the fault of Mexican workers themselves.[44] While many appreciated the area's dependence on labor from Mexico, they justified their low wages. As one local author wrote in 1956, "One outstanding fact, generally admitted, is that the Imperial

Valley would not be the Magic Land that it is today without having had available help from across the border." She characterized the "help" as "stoop labor[ers]" from Mexico, while highlighting that they received "several times" the wage they would have gotten in their "native land."[45]

While there's no doubt cross-boundary wage differentials were (and still are) very substantial,[46] there's also little question that the wages paid to Mexican workers were poverty-level and were significantly less than they would have been for white and native-born workers. But the Valley's ruling elite justified such wages in the name of reining in costs and Mexican laborers' alleged willingness to work for relatively little. As an agribusiness executive from the Imperial Valley asserted, "Large scale production would be impossible without Mexican field labor. Without the Mexicans, costs would be increased 50 per cent." Another person tied into the Valley's agricultural interests stated: "Mexican labor is good labor, and we couldn't get any other class of labor for anything like the same money. . . . Mexicans are good workers under supervision. They appreciate recognition, a small gift, and recognition of their national holidays."[47]

Given the socioeconomic realities associated with such opinion—such as what John Steinbeck characterized as "starvation wages"[48]—Mexican workers in the Valley organized to improve their working conditions. Inspired by the emancipatory promises of the Mexican Revolution[49]—for instance, the notion that land should belong to those who work it—and influenced by anarcho-syndicalists movements emanating from within Mexico—ones that had a strong binational presence[50]—as well as active ties with the U.S.-based Industrial Workers of the World (or "Wobblies"), many workers in the area and throughout the Southwest were attracted to radical politics. Indeed, numerous American anarchists and leftists fought on the side of the so-called Magonistas—the ragtag army of the Mexican Liberal Party led by Ricardo Flores Magón—which attacked, took, and held Mexicali for a few months in early 1911.[51]

For such reasons, much of Mexican-American politics in the early decades of the twentieth century was radical in nature. At the same time, many were involved in relatively conservative forms of politics and worked closely with the Mexican government (via local consulates), which had an interest in preventing radical tendencies from arising in the case of a massive deportation of workers back to Mexico. Local Mexican community organizations, called *mutualistas*, frequently facilitated labor organizing, and their memberships often overlapped with those of labor unions.

Large-scale and ideologically diverse unionization efforts emerged about the time of the Great Depression, a period during which the labor market was flooded with workers because of the economic downturn and during which the power of farmers was growing. The years 1928–34 saw numerous strikes in the Valley, ones of varying levels of duration and militancy. Some were ethnically based, while others—especially those infused with radical left politics (facilitated significantly by the organizing of the Communist Party, the Wobblies having largely disappeared by this time owing to government repression and internal splits)—involved, and built upon, ties between Mexican, Filipino, Anglo, and black workers.

Perhaps the largest labor action was a general strike in January 1934 of five thousand lettuce and vegetable workers; demands included a wage increase from twenty-two and one-half cents per hour to thirty-five cents and toilets in the fields. Following a pattern of behavior in California, local, county, and state authorities ignored constitutional guarantees and engaged in mass arrests, tear-gas raids on peaceful gatherings, beatings, illegal search and seizures, kidnappings, prolonged detentions, and injunctions against picketing, as ways of defeating the strike. In addition, they threatened deportation of pro-union workers of Mexican origin. Local officials expanded their ranks by deputizing growers and vigilantes or by allowing them to act with impunity. These armed goons—the most violent drawn from the local chapters of the Ku Klux Klan, the American Legion, and the fascist Silver Shirts—intimidated workers, burned down the living quarters of some strikers and their families, and beat up journalists and legal advocates, all of which they facilitated by whipping up anticommunist hysteria and a general climate of lawlessness. Reporting on the violence, the January 15, 1934 issue of the *Los Angeles Times* stated: "It's a secret, but the vigilantes are really Legionnaires, and do they have fun!"[52]

Eventually the repression, combined with ongoing efforts by the Mexican government to recruit Mexican workers into conservative unions, broke the strike.[53] The defeat, combined with ongoing repression and the effects of the depression on employment, weakened the hand of the workers and undermined independent unionism, reinforcing a situation in the Valley in which the growers called the shots and agricultural workers subsisted in poverty conditions. As Carey McWilliams, the great California chronicler and analyst wrote of the Valley in 1949, "Today as yesterday, the valley is ruled by a set of power-drunk ruthless nabobs who exploit farm labor with the same savagery they exploit the natural resources of the valley."[54] In 1936, John Steinbeck characterized the large growers' way of rule there—illustrative, he suggests, of much of California's agricultural economy—as one that included "a system of terrorism that would be unusual in the Fascist nations of the world."[55]

The beginning in 1942 of the Bracero Program[56]—a joint U.S.-Mexico government-sponsored contract-labor program championed by U.S. agribusiness that brought millions of Mexican male workers to the United States over its twenty-two years of existence—was a further blow to labor-organizing efforts in California. (Along with Texas, California was the major recipient of braceros.) The presence of the contract workers significantly undercut the ability of farmworkers to organize. Strike efforts in 1951 and 1952 by the National Farm Labor Union in the Imperial Valley's cantaloupe fields—part of an effort to limit the ability of growers throughout California to use braceros and unauthorized migrant workers to undercut organized labor—for example, fell short as the growers had so many braceros that they were able to shift them around to replace striking workers and defeat the strikers.[57]

Eventually, however, workers and their allies figured out how to get around this obstacle. In 1960, the Agricultural Workers Organizing Committee (AWOC) launched a massive strike in the Imperial Valley in which braceros played a supportive role. The Mexican government—which, at the time, still had some progressive strands emanating from the revolutionary heritage of the Institutional Revolutionary Party (PRI)—had inserted a stipulation into the bracero agreements with Washington, D.C. that braceros could not work on any establishment where there was a strike. AWOC took advantage of this clause and would call strikes where there were mixed crews. It was in this vein that AWOC, in conjunction with the United Packinghouse Workers of America, called a strike in the Imperial Valley lettuce fields during December 1960 and January 1961. Even though the workers lost the strike—one that involved violence on both sides[58] (but, as always, much more so on the part of the growers and their proxies)—it was so disruptive to the growers that it contributed to the end of the Bracero Program. Because of the strike, and other pressures, the growers came to see the Bracero Program as insufficiently advantageous. It sent a message to the growers that the status quo was no longer tenable.[59]

These organizing efforts in the Valley contributed to the birth of the United Farm Workers (UFW), which grew rapidly in size and stature in the region. By 1969, César Chávez and the UFW were able to hold a nine-day march from the Coachella Valley to Calexico in support of a strike in the Imperial Valley's big vineyards.[60]

Yet, as before, the growers refused to resign themselves to working with the union. As one analyst wrote, the Valley's growers liked negotiating with the UFW "about as much as a plague of grasshoppers."[61] As such, they worked hard to reverse the workers' gains and to prevent any additional ones. Matters came to a head in late 1978 when the lettuce contract expired and the growers balked at the UFW's demands. This led to a January 1979 lettuce strike, one

Calexico, California, U.S.A. June 2004. We met this family three months after the father had been deported to Mexico. Since then the family had been meeting daily at the wall. A year later, we discovered that U.S. authorities had put a layer of mesh along the steel bars in this area to greatly reduce physical contact through the barrier.

involving more than 3,500 pickers and leading to the traditional divides in the Valley between whites and Latinos, owners, managers, and workers. The strike quickly turned ugly and violent as the growers employed undocumented workers and schoolchildren, among others, as scabs. Fistfights, rock throwing, and various forms of sabotage occurred on a daily basis. Matters intensified when striking workers began entering the fields to talk with strikebreakers or to chase them away. Local police and private security responded by firing tear gas and clubbing the workers in one incident. In another, a guard shot Rufino Contreras in the face, killing the 28-year-old union member.[62] Between seven and eight thousand people filled the streets of Calexico four days later on February 14, 1979, walking three miles to the cemetery where Contreras was buried. Joining César Chávez and UFW cofounder Dolores Huerta was California Governor Jerry Brown. The strike eventually spread throughout the state. Nonetheless, it proved to be the last major action of the United Farm Workers in the Imperial Valley; today the union is effectively nonexistent there. The UFW's old office, located a few dozen yards north of the boundary wall, is now a gathering place for laborers waiting for work.[63]

—◆—

Today, there are no unions for farmworkers in the Imperial Valley. And few of the Valley's agricultural laborers actually live on the U.S. side of the boundary. Instead, most of them reside in Mexico. Such cross-boundary ties manifest the very origins of Mexicali. In some ways, it is the mirror image of Calexico; in others, it is the proverbial other side of the tracks.

Like the Imperial Valley, the Mexicali Valley was a site of speculation. Guillermo Andrade, a Mexican businessman—most of whose commercial associates were from the United States—obtained the colonization rights to the Mexicali Valley in the last years of the nineteenth century and was thus able to control almost all of the area and its resources. Andrade's business dealings were decisive in shaping the Imperial Valley's, as well as greater Mexicali's, birth and early development. Indeed, Rockwood and the California Development Company had to buy 100,000 acres of land from Andrade to secure the land south of the boundary needed for the diversion of water that would irrigate the Imperial Valley. What Andrade got out of the deal—in addition to money—was a promise of enough water to irrigate more than 600,000 acres that he owned south of the divide.[64]

Mexicali originated as a Mexican subsidiary of the Colorado River Land Company, owned by a syndicate of businessmen from Los Angeles, one headed by Harrison Otis Gray, publisher of the *Los Angeles Times*, and his son-in-law, Harry Chandler. The California-Mexico Land and Cattle Company, that subsidiary, originally focused on livestock raising, but with the advent of irrigation that mimicked the development just across the boundary in the Imperial Valley, it leased lands to farmers who produced cotton in the area. The syndicate bought up an enormous amount of land—850,000 acres—much of it agriculturally productive. Because it was established as a Mexican land-development corporation, the Colorado River Land Company was able to circumvent legal prohibitions against non-Mexican nationals owning land near the U.S. boundary.[65]

Many of the settlers in Mexicali's early years were Chinese. Entrepreneurs from China began arriving in Baja California Norte in the late 1800s, but Chinese migration to the area did not really take off until the arrival of irrigation. The Mexican government, appreciative of the area's great economic potential and desirous to effectively lay claim to its border region, actively encouraged people to settle the area. Mexican nationals found the region to be of little attraction, however, so Mexico felt compelled to facilitate Chinese immigration instead. The imposition of the Chinese Exclusion Act in the United States in 1882 also facilitated the arrival and settlement of Chinese in the borderlands as many tried to enter the United States from Mexico—and from Canada as well. At the same time, Mexican citizenship or residency allowed individuals of Chinese origin in the late 1800s to cross into the United States with relative ease, a situation that lasted until roughly 1902.[66] From 1910 to 1921, Baja California Norte's Chinese population increased more than sixfold, reaching a total of 2,806. By 1927, it would more than double, reaching almost six thousand. Much of that population was concentrated in Mexicali: one-third of the city's population in 1930 was Chinese, with most located in a large commercial and residential district in eastern Mexicali, which is still known today as *La Chinesca*. It was also about this time, however, that the Chinese population began to precipitously decline as a result of the Great Depression. The economic downturn—combined with the arrival in Mexicali of large numbers of Mexican workers forcibly repatriated from the United States—led to significant unemployment. The sudden crash of cotton prices in 1928, for example, led many Chinese farmworkers to leave the region. The downturn—which had a devastating effect on Mexicali—also helped give rise to nativist movements within the area (as well as elsewhere in Mexico), resulting in Mexican attacks on foreign-owned businesses, the majority of which were Chinese. Such attacks, combined with plummeting economic fortune, forced many Chinese to leave—with some going elsewhere in Mexico and Latin America and a small number drifting across the boundary to the United States, but most returning to China. By 1940, there were only 618 Chinese, according to the census, in the entire state of Baja California Norte.[67]

In the run-up to this time, an agrarian movement of Mexican

farmers in the Mexicali Valley was demanding that productive land be owned by Mexicans, with many calling for the expropriation of the lands of the Colorado River Land Company and their redistribution to their compatriots. The terms of the agreement by which the company had originally acquired the land required it to colonize the area with Mexican settlers, but by 1936 it still owned or controlled 95 percent of the land. Over the next decade, about half the company's holdings were either sold or expropriated by the federal government to make *ejidos*—communal farms in the form of large territories that surrounded already existing settlements and which were formally granted to them for the use by their residents.[68] In 1946, the government purchased the company's remaining land, further laying the foundation for a population boom as many Mexicans arrived in the region in the hope of gaining access to the redistributed land.[69]

Like other border towns, Mexicali's initial growth owes much to its rise as a center of vice for residents on the U.S. side of the international boundary. Mexicali came to be a regional center of casinos, opium dens, brothels, saloons, and dance halls—principally because of the activities of the governor of Baja California Norte, Esteban Cantú, who encouraged and regulated vice-related operations as a way to raise capital for investments in public works and education in Mexicali and Tijuana and to maintain political autonomy from Mexico City.[70] The sanctioning by the Mexican government in 1908 of gambling in Baja California facilitated such commercial activities and led to a significant influx of U.S. investment and tourists.

Developments in the United States also greatly fueled Mexicali's vice industry. Reforms associated with the Progressive and World War I eras led to "dry" and red-light-eradication laws, leading U.S. business people engaging in vice to go to Canada, Cuba, and Mexico for opportunities. The efforts of the reformist movement in California to impose its puritanical notions of morality and religion on the state's population from 1900 to 1920 greatly intensified the flow toward Mexico.[71] Soon Mexicali came to be associated with saloon culture, red-light Chinatown ambience, and the blurring of the lines of class, race, nationality, and gender as people of all types rubbed shoulders in the city's clubs near the boundary crossing with Calexico. As early as 1909, Mexico's consul in Calexico complained that cantinas, cabarets, and cafés constituted 75 percent of Mexicali's economy.[72]

But Mexicali's vice aspects were quickly taken over by its demographic and agricultural boom. The departure of most Chinese, the mass expulsion of Mexicans from the United States during the Great Depression, and the gradual transfer of all the Colorado River Land Company's land—through a combination of sales by the company and expropriation by the government—greatly aided in the "Mexicanization" of the Mexicali Valley. From 1940 to 1950, the town of Mexicali's population exploded from 18,755 inhabitants to 65,000. The Bracero Program further contributed to Mexicali's growth as thousands of would-be braceros flocked to the border region. Many never crossed the boundary, but stayed in Mexicali. Many others did cross and became workers in the United States, but their families settled on the Mexico side of the line. By 1950, not only was Mexicali the second-most populous Mexican border town, the Mexicali Valley was the country's third-largest cotton-producing region and its fifth-largest source of exports.[73]

The Mexicali region continued to experience huge growth in the second half of the twentieth century in the face of a rapid rise in the size and importance of its industrial and commercial sectors and the decline of its agricultural sector. This coincided with the decline of the Bracero Program and the opening of Mexicali's first maquiladora—an assembly plant producing exclusively for export—in 1962. With the establishment of Mexico's Border Industrialization Program—the intention of which was to create local magnets for economic growth in the borderlands and reduce the region's high unemployment levels—the maquiladora industry took off. While Mexicali's maquiladoras never approached the number of Tijuana, it is now third among border cities with such factories, which numbered 137 in 2006.[74]

Today, Mexicali is also the third-largest city in Mexico's northern border region, with a population of approximately 900,000.[75] It dwarfs its neighbor across the boundary, Calexico, the population of which is only about 37,000 inhabitants. In some ways, Calexico seems like an appendage or a suburb of Mexicali and distinct from the rest of the Imperial Valley. In other ways, Calexico and, even more so, the American valley of which it is part seem like a gated community on a proverbial hill surrounded by the threatening masses below—or, in this case, across the line—on whom its residents depend in all sorts of ways and whom many of them simultaneously fear.[76]

—◇◇◇—

Like many twinned border towns, Calexico and Mexicali cooperate in a number of areas. The towns had such strong economic and social ties in the 1920s that their respective fire departments answered calls in either town.[77] Still today, Calexico's fire department occasionally responds to emergencies in Mexicali. Meanwhile many children from Mexicali cross the boundary on a daily basis to attend private schools in Calexico, as do about 60,000 middle-class Mexicans with U.S. government-issued border-crossing cards in order to shop at Calexico businesses ranging from five-and-dime stores to Wal-Mart, providing a huge impetus to the local economy.[78] At the same time, many Imperial Valley residents cross into Mexicali on weekends to enjoy the city's Chinese restaurants or dance clubs. And notwithstanding the presence of the international boundary, ethnocultural boundaries are quite blurry. An estimated 80 percent of Calexico's children, for example, enter the city's school system speaking Spanish, and approximately 95 percent of its residents are Latino.[79]

Such fuzziness across the boundary presents significant challenges for U.S authorities policing the divide. Because Calexico's downtown abuts the international line, it is relatively easy for boundary jumpers to blend into Calexico's surroundings. At the same time, numerous residents feel sympathy for unauthorized crossers and provide them with food and water, or hide them in their homes. Others, drawn by the lucrative nature of smuggling, shelter migrants for a price. For such reasons, many in the area refuse to cooperate with the United States Border Patrol.[80]

Despite such boundary blurring and interdependency across the international line, the contemporary relationship between Mexicali and the Imperial Valley is far from an equal or just one, an outcome facilitated by the very presence of the U.S.-Mexico divide. Reminiscent of South Africa's dependence on "homelands" for its workforce,[81] the Imperial Valley today draws much of its manual labor from across the boundary. As of 1998, half of Imperial County's total workforce of 40,000 lived on the Mexican side of the international line, in and around Mexicali. Seventy percent of these boundary crossers worked in agriculture and made up 88 percent of the sector's workforce.[82] It was estimated in 2001 that about 15,000 such workers crossed into Calexico during the peak harvest on a daily basis. These laborers, who typically have work visas, usually arrive by 4:00 a.m. From there, labor contractors transport them to farms, some as far way as Yuma, Arizona—sixty miles to the east. And they return home to the Mexican side of the boundary at the end of the day. Working conditions, as throughout much of California agriculture, remain poor. Workers are frequently paid less than the minimum wage or only paid for some of the hours they work. Sometimes they are not paid for weeks' worth of work. Growers insulate themselves from accountability for these legal violations by largely and increasingly relying on labor contractors, rather than directly employing workers themselves.[83] As the Valley's economy has diversified over the last decade and agriculture has declined in relative importance, labor contractors today sometimes have trouble finding a sufficient number of workers as there are many crossers who prefer to work in the Valley's growing service and construction sectors.[84]

In addition to helping to bring about an apartheid-like labor market, the boundary between Mexicali and Calexico also serves as a site for geographically divided loved ones to come together. On an almost daily basis, one can witness families, husbands and wives, and lovers talking, touching hands, and exchanging kisses and hugs through the narrow spaces of the steel posts that form part of the boundary wall that now scars the local landscape. Holidays such as Mother's Day are especially popular for these encounters. Although such reunions are not supposed to take place, Border Patrol agents, while carefully watching them, typically do not prohibit them.[85]

But perhaps nothing embodies the complex nature of the ties between the Imperial and Mexicali valleys more than a key source of their modern development: engineered water.[86]

Settlers in the Imperial Valley began clamoring in the early 1920s for irrigation water free of any Mexican control and its associated problems. One such problem was the loss of water through seepage and evaporation owing to the canal's ill-defined banks within Mexico. A greater one was the heavy costs of flood control associated with the canal—the lion's share of which (including on the Mexican side of the line) was paid for by the Imperial Valley and its residents. That most of the land in Mexico protected by the controls was owned by the Los Angeles–based Colorado River Land Company only added fuel to the fires of anger burning in the hearts of the Imperial Valley's inhabitants. And as was so often the case in conflicts in the region, matters of race and nation were at the fore.

Because the company leased much of their land to Mexican, Japanese, and, especially, Chinese farmers in the Mexicali Valley, farmers in the Imperial Valley accused it of providing water which rightfully belonged to "red-blooded, free Americans" to "Japs and Chinamen." Open racism was the order of the day. As W. H. Brooks, a member of the Imperial County Board of Supervisors, asked in 1919, "Who wants to drink water from a stream when he knows that there are 7,000 Chinamen, Japs, and Mexicans camped on that stream a few miles above in Mexico?"[87]

More than anything else, it was the growing quantity of the Colorado's water consumed on the Mexican side that concerned farmers in the Imperial Valley as the amount of land under irrigation grew dramatically, largely owing to cotton production—this at a time when the Imperial Valley's own population, agricultural production, and thus thirst for water were skyrocketing. It was in this context that the call for a canal located entirely within the United States—an "All-American Canal"—was born.[88] While most people in the Valley embraced the idea, it would take more than a decade for the canal's construction to begin in 1934 because of a variety of factors ranging from opposition from Harry Chandler, by that time, the head of the Colorado River Land Company—fearing what it would mean for his lands in Mexicali—to bureaucratic infighting, to disputes between U.S. states in the Southwest (many of which perceived California as arrogant and corrupt and as a drain on the growth of their own states). Actual water delivery from the eighty-mile canal began in 1940.[89]

Water is today perhaps the primary source of conflict between the two valleys. The Imperial Valley receives the lion's share of the life-giving liquid—despite having only a fraction of the population. That the Colorado River flows north to south—an accident of physical geography—allows the United States to take almost all the water from the river before it reaches Mexico. Indeed, in some years, the riverbed below the California-Mexico boundary runs dry. It is for such reasons that Mexicali farmers now protest a U.S. government plan to concretize the remaining twenty-three-mile, unlined portion of the canal (so that San Diego will have more water for its growing population and consumption): in 2006, seepage from the unlined portion of the canal into wells on Mexico's side of the boundary provided water to about 25,000 people, including 400 farmers.[90]

Calexico, California, U.S.A. June 2004. Portions of the All-American Canal hug the boundary between the United States and Mexico.

If waters divide the United States and Mexico, they also link them—often in perverse ways.

The New and Alamo rivers that flow northward from Mexicali through the Imperial Valley create a toxic connection. The New River, for example, has often been characterized as North America's most polluted waterway. In April 1994, the *Imperial Valley Press* reported that a truck carrying sewage fell off a bridge into the river. After twenty-four hours, when a wrecker pulled the truck out, the paint covering the truck was gone. Local officials decided that the truck's cargo of sewage need not be recovered because it posed no threat to the river.[91] Another newspaper report characterizes it as "a ditch carrying drainage water the color of pea soup that brims with sewage, animal carcasses and industrial waste from Mexicali. This toxic stew contains bacteria and viruses known to cause tuberculosis, polio, hepatitis and typhoid."[92]

The two rivers carry their load into the Salton Sea, a low-lying area at the northern end of the Imperial Valley. While it was once part of a sea that covered the entire area millions of years ago, it owes its present-day existence to the tendency of Mother Nature to fight back against attempts to tame the formidable Colorado River:[93] a massive flood during 1905–1907 brought about by huge rains and a poorly designed cut in an irrigation canal together made the river overflow its banks, almost destroying the towns of Calexico and Mexicali in the process. Since that time, it has largely been agricultural runoff from the Mexicali and Imperial valleys that has maintained what is perhaps more appropriately characterized as a large lake, the shore around which is the site of a stunningly failed real estate development scheme—symptomatic of classic California speculation.[94] It was to this area, U.S. authorities guessed, that Julio César Gallegos and the other members of his group were headed—in the hope of meeting up with someone who would drive them to Los Angeles.

Just as the area's desert and waters give life, they bring about death. While most of the bacteria emanating from the Mexican side of the boundary are gone by the time the rivers reach the area, the Salton Sea has extremely high levels of salinity and pollutants owing to agricultural runoff and overirrigation.[95] As such, recent years have seen massive die-offs of fish and birds on the water's surface.[96] And although the Colorado River-born waters of the All-American Canal, much of which hugs the Mexico boundary, are much cleaner, they also kill: many migrants, not having anything to grab onto along the concretized sides, not knowing how to swim or fooled by the seemingly tranquil appearance of the channel's swift flow, have drowned while trying to traverse its waters as part of an effort to beat the U.S. government's ever-tightening immigration and boundary enforcement web.[97] Twenty-six people drowned in the canal's waters in 2000 alone. Such a manner of death seems "supremely ironic," writes journalist Ken Ellingwood. "Where else but California could you drown in the middle of the desert?"[98]

Some of the dead—the unidentified ones—end up in Holtville, one of the Imperial Valley's original towns and one notable in the early decades of the twentieth century for the tiny size of its Mexico-origin population. In 1927, the town only had one Mexican property owner, a single restaurant proprietor, and only a handful of Mexican residents. One of the reasons given at the time for the paucity of Mexicans—according to Anglos and Mexicans alike—was the especially strong racial antipathy of the town's residents.[99]

Today, life in Holtville, a small town of about six thousand, is a different story. Like the valley as a whole, a strong majority of its residents are Latino. On the outskirts of the quiet agricultural town that advertises itself as the "Carrot Capital of the World" is the Terrace Park Cemetery, the back of which is a dirt-covered potter's field—the burial site of the poor, destitute, and unidentified. Dead migrants whose identity the coroner is not able to ascertain end up buried there. Their grave markers are simple, small concrete slabs engraved with "John Doe" or "Jane Doe." As of February 2006, the bodies of an estimated four hundred unidentified migrants lay there.[100]

Holtville's "residents"—dead and alive—say a great deal about the making of the Imperial and Mexicali valleys and the territorial division that separates them. As long as there is a place called the United States and one called Mexico, a boundary between the two is inevitable. What is not given is the nature of that divide. That is the ongoing product of myriad forces—political-economic, sociocultural, and geographical. It is the nature of the boundary that determines who can cross into the United States from Mexico, under what conditions, and how and where.

———

The Imperial Valley was never as central to the processes involved in the making of the U.S.-Mexico boundary as were more populous border cities such as San Diego, but it has always been an inextricable part of them in terms of both cause and effect. The social divisions that are inherently linked to the territorial divide have been involved in the making of the Imperial Valley since Anglos first settled the area around 1900. Nonetheless, the newness of the boundary as a line of control and the largely unencumbered flow of people and goods across the line in the Valley's early years presented U.S. authorities with myriad challenges.

In 1918, for example, A. A. Musgrave, inspector in charge of the Immigration Service in Calexico, wrote of how the trials of policing the boundary in that area were greater than most places given that "the business associations between Calexico and other American towns" in the Valley and places "south of the line in Mexicali are so numerous and on such a large scale." Moreover, they covered "such a large extent of territory adjacent to the border." The small number of authorities, the flat, physical expanse, and the presence of people throughout the area meant, he asserted, that "any person crossing could soon mingle with, or among, the ranch people and workmen, making the tracing of their movements quite difficult." That there were only five immigration officers in the area who spent most of their time dealing with customs matters and who were not on post at night made it even easier.[101]

Such factors, combined with the newness of the boundary (and national territorial delimitations more broadly) as a line of control meant that residents had to be "taught" how to accept and embrace the line and those individuals and practices that gave it life. A 1927 editorial from the *Imperial Valley Press*, for instance, effectively attempted to instruct its readers how to react to the newly established United States Border Patrol. It urged them to help in the fight against "ineligible aliens" who entered the United States through "the back door" as such people are "nine times out of ten the kind of alien that Uncle Sam does not want." Consequently, the newspaper called upon Valley residents to "aid the border patrol in its good work by stopping promptly [when asked], answering questions put to them and letting the government men see that they have the support of American citizens in keeping out those who are not wanted."[102]

Given the deep divides of race, class, and nation in the Valley, it does not seem that it took much to bring about cooperation from "Americans"—which was largely synonymous with Anglo—on such matters. Indeed, boundary policing writ large took place not just along the line that divided Calexico from Mexicali, but in locations throughout the Valley. As a man from East Los Angeles recalling the repeated humiliation his father endured as someone of Mexican origin living and working in southern California recounted, "In 1949, we were driving back from Mexicali, where my grandfather lived, and we tried to go into a restaurant in Westmorland [a town about thirty miles north of Calexico] . . . There was a sign at the door: 'No Dogs or Mexicans Allowed.'"[103]

At the boundary itself, racial policing was also at work. As elsewhere along the international line, Chinese people were subjects of concern in the early decades of the 1900s. In the 1930s, for instance, U.S. immigration officials in the area of Calexico closely monitored events in Mexicali when an anti-Chinese movement arose there in the context of the Great Depression. (Chinese exclusion was still in effect in the United States.) On at least one occasion, U.S. officials in Calexico communicated to members of the "Liga Nacionalista Mexicana" that they would lose the right to enter the United States if their actions helped to precipitate an exodus of Chinese in Mexicali northward across the boundary.[104]

But it was as a regulator of labor that the U.S.-Mexico boundary was most useful to—and necessary for—the Imperial Valley's ruling class. As early as 1928, growers threatened striking workers with deportation if they did not return to work, and succeeded in getting some union organizers deported to Mexico.[105] This appears to have been a common tactic in the decades that followed.[106]

Although the Imperial Valley economy clearly benefited from the plentiful availability of unauthorized labor, it did not prevent many in the area from contending that unsanctioned migrants were a detriment to the U.S. socioeconomic fabric and a security threat as well. A 1951 *Life* magazine article, for example, acknowledged that "most growers welcome wetbacks" and reported that they made up half of the Valley's workforce at the time. Praising their work, the magazine characterized the typical "wetback" as someone who "can weed a 1,000-foot furrow without once straightening up." "[H]e willingly works," the piece continued, "with the short-handled hoe which, so much more efficient around delicate plants, tortures American spines." Yet, it also argued that "[wetbacks] depress wage rates, lower living standards, take money out of the U.S. and unwittingly furnish protective cover for more dangerous aliens to sneak into the country," while characterizing the influx as a "silent invasion by a Mexican army." Although the United States Border Patrol tried to stop unauthorized entries, "its most valiant efforts [were] exasperatingly futile," the report asserted. It was for such reasons that the immigration force of southeastern California (which includes the Valley)—then numbering around ninety, according to *Life*—had asked for one hundred additional agents.[107]

In the months preceding Operation Wetback—a massive round-up and deportation of migrants in 1954—Imperial County officials clamored about the alleged expenses of unauthorized migrants to the Valley. An April 1954 article on the matter reported their claim that "illegal temporary residents" cost the county at least $150,000 per year in terms of healthcare, welfare, and imprisonment. Asking if there was some way "the state or Federal government could reimburse Imperial County for its disproportionately high police, hospital, and welfare costs," officials called upon California's governor to take remedial action, leading him to appeal to the Eisenhower administration for help. Helping to justify such efforts, the report characterized the Border Patrol as "pitifully undermanned" while asserting that "no one could guess how many Communist agents, saboteurs, and international smugglers were infiltrating the country through the mesh of holes in the border." In terms of enforcement infrastructure along the boundary between the Imperial and Mexicali Valleys, only six and a half of the ninety miles of the divide had fencing at the time, making the rest of the boundary in the area "sheer imagination."[108]

By the 1990s, when Julio César Gallegos journeyed to California, the enforcement apparatus along the boundary was far more substantial than it had been in the 1950s. Still, it had come to be increasingly seen by many in the United States as a dangerously porous divide. Just as the New River carries unhealthy pollutants into the United States, unauthorized migration, many argued—as many contend today—is a threat to the country's sociocultural and political-economic fabric, and to the physical safety of its inhabitants. And for this reason, they said, the boundary had to be made be "real" so that it would be an effective barrier (in addition to a gateway for welcome

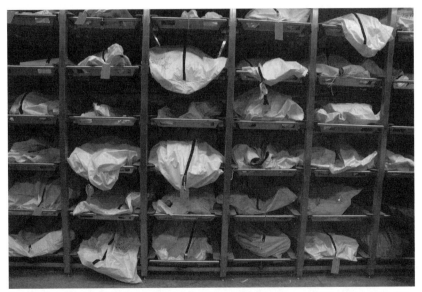

Tucson, Arizona, U.S.A. October 2005. Migrant bodies among the corpses in the morgue of the Pima County Medical Examiner's Office. The office is responsible for identifying and conducting autopsies on the migrants found in the desert. Because of the steep rise in migrant deaths in the Arizona border region, the office had to rent a refrigerated semitrailer to expand their storage space in July 2005.

goods, services, and crossers) to unauthorized migrants and other undesirables, rather than a mere line in the middle of a gradual zone of transition between the two countries. Such calls led to a dramatic transformation of the boundary between the time Gallegos first traveled to California in 1993, and 1998 when he died while traversing the border region that unites and separates Mexico and the United States.

Jacumba, California,
U.S.A. and Jacume,
Baja California Norte,
Mexico. March 2001.

THREE **THE BORDER**

CONSUELO DURÁN, JULIO'S MOTHER and the last partner of his father, Florentino Gallegos (they never formally married), died in 1993. Like Don Florentino, she had children from a previous marriage, and her spouse had died. According to Jackie, Julio's wife, Doña Consuelo passed away in her youngest son's arms at their home in central Mexico. ("Doña" is a term of respect in Spanish-speaking countries for older women. "Don" is the masculine version.) His mother's death devastated Julio. Combined with the limited economic opportunities in his hometown and the fact that his older brother and half siblings lived in Los Angeles, her passing away led him to decide soon thereafter to leave his place of birth and join the rest of his family in the United States.

Don Florentino, who had long had permanent residency status in the United States, but, having retired, was by then spending the majority of his time in Mexico, accompanied Julio for most of the journey. He brought his son to Tijuana in 1993, where, through relatives living in the border city, he found a *coyote*, a professional smuggler, as Julio did not have papers to enter the United States.

That first trip to Los Angeles was supposed to cost $300. After getting him across the line and leading him all the way to L.A., however, the guide brought him back to Tijuana. As far as Don Florentino could recall, it was because the guide lost the address where he was supposed to bring Julio. So he didn't have to pay the smuggler.

Instead, Don Florentino, who was already in Los Angeles by that time, went south to Tijuana and bought a false *mica*, or identity card—in this case, a "green card" as the identity document for permanent, non-U.S citizen residents is called—for only 50 pesos (about $5 at the time). According to Don Florentino, the fake *mica* was a lousy imitation. Nevertheless, it worked. Don Florentino walked through the San Ysidro (southern San Diego), California port of entry first with his official U.S. government-issued identity document. Julio followed right behind, showing his newly purchased counterfeit card.

Tijuana, Baja California Norte, Mexico. March 2001. Here at Las Playas, Tijuana, the wall slices into the Pacific Ocean.

That Julio was able to cross in 1993 with the ease with which he did was perhaps due to luck or an inexperienced immigration inspector. But it was also in many ways a sign of the times, one of relatively lax enforcement, an era that would soon end as radical transformations of the boundary policing apparatus were on the horizon—as the difficulties he encountered in 1998 tragically demonstrated. That said, it is incorrect to draw the conclusion that crossing the boundary without authorization was an easy affair until the changes initiated beginning in 1994 during the first years of the Clinton administration. To the contrary: the very making of the U.S.-Mexico boundary and the larger border region has always involved the effective deployment of power to include and exclude, and of violence—both physical and structural; it has thus always had life-and-death implications. This was as true in 1848 when the international divide was first delineated as it is today.

Nonetheless, the nature of the divide between Mexico and the United States has changed dramatically over the more than 150 years since it was established in its present geographical expression. There was nothing inevitable about these changes. Just as things were once radically different in the U.S.-Mexico borderlands,[1] how matters unfolded to reach the point that Julio faced near the end of the 1990s was far from preordained. Yet a boundary such as that which now exists between the United States and Mexico makes a lot of sense in that it reflects and reproduces the logic of a world of nation-states, which require physical lines that delimit and define national space and, thus, "us" and "them" and "our" territory and "theirs."

The stronger these geographical and social categories are, the more formidable are the boundaries between them, as is the tendency of those championing the boundaries to embrace neat categorizations that are belied by a messy reality. As the case of the U.S.-Mexico boundary and the associated border region has always demonstrated, "us" and "them," "here" and "there" have always been united, just as they have been divided. Indeed, the very making of the United States and the making of Mexico implicated (and still do) processes that involve actors and processes emanating from either side of the line and beyond.[2] Burying and forgetting that messy, transboundary reality, while in other ways embracing it, is a necessary part of the creation of the boundary in a world of both supposedly self-contained nation-states and social relations that transcend national territory. This helps explain why the boundary simultaneously serves as both an obstacle and a gateway— functions that are both contradictory and complementary.

The specifics of the U.S.-Mexico boundary's contradictions and accompanying complements are manifestations of the manner in which the boundary was born: via war and conquest, processes inextricably related to the making of the categories of race, class, and nation present in the making of California's Imperial Valley, the larger border region, and the United States as a whole. These categories necessarily involve hierarchy, exclusion and inclusion, and reflect and further the interests of certain groups over others. But they also necessarily involve interactions among individuals and places along the attendant hierarchies. In this regard, the boundary has always been not only about who belongs and who does not, and thus who gets what, but also about the terms on which people and places from either side of the line relate to one another.

—⁓—

While the origins of the U.S.-Mexico divide are found in the imperial competition between Spain, France, and England for "possessions" in North America, it was Napoléon's 1803 sale of "Louisiana" to the United States for $15 million that put Washington on an eventual collision course with Mexico. Almost immediately after the signing of the treaty concluding the sale, U.S. President

Thomas Jefferson foreshadowed U.S. expansionist designs on what would become Mexico, expressing the view that Louisiana included all lands north and east of the Rio Grande, thus laying claim to Spanish settlements such as San Antonio and Santa Fe.[3]

Jefferson's claim was a manifestation of, among other things, a much larger problem: namely, a lack of agreement between imperial France, England, and Spain over the location of the boundaries separating their territories in North America. This led to disagreement between the United States and Spain over Texas. While the two countries eventually entered into negotiations to resolve their differences, the United States invaded eastern Florida (which was then part of New Spain) in 1818 to force Spain's hand. Under the terms of the Adams-Onís Treaty of 1819, Spain agreed to exchange East Florida and West Florida (today the southern parts of the states of Mississippi and Alabama, and the entire state of Florida, respectively) for U.S. recognition of an international boundary between Texas and Louisiana as well as monetary compensation—which it never received. But despite U.S. gains, many Americans were unhappy that the United States had not acquired Texas as well. They argued that the true location of the boundary of what was previously known as the Louisiana territory under the French was—or at least should be—the Rio Grande.[4]

Such claims were symptomatic of a body of thought and practice that came to be known as "Manifest Destiny," a term coined by writer John O'Sullivan in 1839. Manifest destiny embodied ideas of Anglo-Saxon superiority and racism, combined with an expansionist ideology that embraced a view of the United States as a beneficent power with a right and duty to conquer other lands and peoples. As Walt Whitman proclaimed in 1846 in championing efforts to seize Mexican territory, "Miserable, inefficient Mexico—what has she to do with the great mission of peopling the New World with a noble race? Be it ours to achieve this mission!"[5]

Such a worldview has deep roots in American political culture—going all the way back to the Puritans.[6] Even later, in 1767, for instance, Benjamin Franklin had named Mexico and Cuba as territories for future expansion by what would soon be the United States of America.[7] Thomas Jefferson, among other prominent Americans, held a similar viewpoint.[8]

When Mexico gained independence from Spain in 1821, the new country thus acquired the challenge of protecting its northern boundary. This was especially important in terms of Texas since many in the United States still claimed the territory as part of the Louisiana Purchase. Nonetheless, Washington extended official recognition of Mexico.

Meanwhile, Mexico had serious difficulty establishing control over Texas, a sparsely populated territory several hundred miles away from the capital city. So the Mexican government had little choice but to continue the Spanish policy of allowing the entry of American settlers. Thousands of proslavery Southerners soon flocked to Texas in search of new lands for the cultivation of cotton and the extension of the slave economy. In 1830, however, Mexico outlawed slavery and prohibited further immigration to Texas, infuriating U.S. slaveholders there as well as those elements of the local Mexican elite who enjoyed the benefits of American capital flowing into the territory. Despite the Mexican government's immigration restrictions, Americans continued to enter Texas. By 1835, there were about 35,000 Anglos and only 5,000 Mexicans in the territory. It soon became clear to the Mexican government that many in the United States had designs on Texas and other parts of Mexico.[9] The relative isolation of Texas, New Mexico, and California from the population centers of Mexico, moreover, facilitated the rise of regionalist tendencies and separatist movements. Nonetheless, Washington avoided attempts to annex Texas forcefully during the 1820s and 1830s, instead opting for diplomatic persuasion and economic incentives— later called "dollar diplomacy"—aimed at convincing Mexico to sell Texas and adjacent territories.[10]

But such efforts became redundant when Anglo-Texans, with help from American funding and volunteers, as well as from some *Tejanos* (Mexican Texans), successfully rebelled against Mexican authorities in 1836. The newly independent Republic of Texas asked the United States to annex it in 1837, but President Andrew Jackson, while very sympathetic to the request, merely recognized its independence. Although demands for Texas's annexation enjoyed wide popular support throughout the United States, there was also opposition, especially from antislavery forces in the Northeast, and Jackson did not want to provoke interregional antagonisms. Thus, it was not until 1845, under proslavery President John Tyler, that the United States annexed Texas, enraging Mexico in the process. And consistent with prior claims, the United States asserted that Texas's territory extended to the Rio Grande, whereas Mexico insisted that the boundary was located 150 miles to the north at the Nueces River.

In early 1846, President James K. Polk, also a supporter of slavery, deliberately provoked Mexico by sending troops to the Rio Grande. (From Mexico's perspective, this constituted an invasion.) Soon thereafter, skirmishes between U.S. and Mexican troops ensued, quickly resulting in full-scale war. In terms of population size, levels of economic development, and military strength, Mexico was seriously outmatched. For two years, the war raged on, largely in favor of the United States.[11] It ended with U.S. troops occupying Mexico City and the signing in February 1848 of the Treaty of Guadalupe Hidalgo by which Mexico ceded about 40 percent of its territory to the United States. Under the treaty's terms, the United States annexed more than five hundred thousand square miles of Mexican land, a territory equivalent in size to that of Western Europe, and absorbed 100,000 Mexican citizens and 200,000 Native Americans living there.[12] As a result of the war, the United States gained land that eventually became all or part of the territory of ten U.S. states: Texas, Arizona, New Mexico, Oklahoma, Wyoming, Colorado, Kansas, Utah, Nevada, and California.[13]

Mexico's loss of so much territory was far from predestined given the complexity of social relations and allegiances, and shifting alliances in the U.S.-Mexico borderlands in the first half of the nineteenth century. Tensions within a newly independent Mexico, between a centralizing state in Mexico City and the forces of decentralization in the country's northern borderlands, certainly facilitated secession and conquest. But these differences could have been resolved had it not been for the powerful pull of the U.S. market—just as they were elsewhere in Mexico. In the period of 1800–1860, the total income of the United States rose 1,270.4 percent, whereas that of Mexico declined 10.5 percent.[14] This had the effect of drawing Mexico's northern borderlands toward the United States and, as a result, facilitating the goals of those championing U.S. territorial expansionism as it weakened the ties between the population of Mexico's northern states and the country's center.[15]

Principal among these goals was to force Mexico to cede California and, to a lesser extent, New Mexico, in addition to consolidating control over Texas so to be able to spread slavery, and to give up additional territory on its northern boundary. California was key because it was such an important source of raw materials for the burgeoning U.S. industrial sector and because it had such lucrative fisheries and strategic harbors. As President James Polk explained to Congress, California's harbors "would afford shelter for our navy, for our numerous whale ships, and other merchant vessels employed in the Pacific ocean, and would in a short period become the marts of an extensive and profitable commerce with China, and other countries of the East."[16]

But such gains proved insufficient for many U.S. expansionists who wanted to maximize the southern extent of the territories of western New Mexico and Arizona for a transcontinental railroad route and access to the rich copper mines in the area of Mesilla (in present-day New Mexico). Inaccuracies in the Treaty of Guadalupe Hidalgo regarding the boundary's precise location between the Mexican state of Chihuahua and New Mexico laid the foundation for tensions. Mexicans and Anglo-Texan and New Mexican cattle ranchers moved into Mesilla, and the governors of Chihuahua and New Mexico both claimed jurisdiction over the area, threatening to send troops to enforce their claims. Substantiating the contention that politics is the continuation of war by other means, the head of a special 1853 delegation sent to Mexico City to resolve the conflict, James Gadsden, made clear that the United States would militarily seize parts of northern Mexico if that country's authorities did not concede to American demands. While expansionists did not get all the lands they sought—the U.S. delegation tried, for example, to compel Mexico to give up several northern states—the United States gained the mineral-rich areas in southern New Mexico as well as the desired lands in Arizona via the so-called Gadsden Purchase.[17]

After the Civil War, American expansionists continued pursuing additional changes in the U.S.-Mexican boundary. This led to further raiding of Mexico from Texas and Southern California by what came to be known as filibusters.[18] As the twentieth century approached, however, Mexico consolidated its holds over its northern territory through significant demographic and economic growth. These changes, along with the construction of a railroad network in the border region, facilitated further development of transboundary ties. Combined with generous concessions granted to foreigners by the Mexican government of Porfirio Díaz that gave many wealthy U.S. business interests control over large swaths of land, and domination over Mexico's oil and mining sectors and much of the country's agri-culture, such developments helped to undermine and lessen remaining filibustering tendencies.[19]

From a U.S. perspective, the most serious challenges in the after-math of the Treaty of Guadalupe Hidalgo involved the subjugation of the populations gained through the war with Mexico: *Mexicanos* and Native Americans. This entailed violence committed by U.S. and local authorities and, among others, Anglo settlers, a common occur-rence in the border region in the second half of the nineteenth and the early twentieth centuries.[20] Anglos sought to dispossess Mexicans as part of the Americanization of the region, a process that unfolded

Imperial Beach, California, U.S.A. September 2005. People gather here daily at what today is called Border Field to meet with loved ones on the other side of the barrier. First Lady Pat Nixon dedicated the site as Friendship Park in 1971. Mrs. Nixon ordered a guard to cut out a section of the then barbed-wire boundary fence. She then embraced Mexican children saying, "I hope there won't be a fence here too long." (Doyle 2004)

unevenly in the annexed territories; not all ethnic Mexicans were immediately swept aside. As historian Benjamin Heber Johnson writes, "Broadly speaking, where ethnic Mexicans remained a majority—in parts of southern California, New Mexico, and the border regions of Texas—they continued to hold significant amounts of land and to wield political power. They therefore avoided becoming a despised and oppressed racial caste."[21] But the gradual and increasing Anglo encroachment into these areas led to the dispossession and disempowerment of the Mexican population there, too, that had already occurred elsewhere in the borderlands, and the violence that these processes often entailed. (The marginalization of the Mexican population proved to be a de facto prerequisite for U.S. statehood for the former Mexican territories. Arizona and New Mexico, given their large and well-situated Mexican population—relative to the size and power of the Anglo populations—thus took much longer to become states than California, which had an Anglo majority by 1850.[22])

Southern Texas was the site of the bloodiest fights as U.S. officials and Anglo settlers clashed with the area's Mexican inhabitants who were resisting the destruction of their livelihoods brought about via the encroaching American political-economic order. In one particularly gory episode that began in 1915, elements of the Mexican-origin population launched raids on Anglo-owned ranches, irrigation works, and railroads. The raids soon coalesced into a full-scale uprising. Armed men—from both sides of the boundary—attacked U.S. post offices, stole livestock, burned railroad bridges, robbed stores, killed farmers, and engaged in pitched battles with local posses, Texas Rangers, and thousands of U.S. soldiers deployed to the border region to quell the uprising. Anglo settlers and local officials reacted to the uprising by launching a far more violent counterinsurgency campaign, one that included systematic harassment of ethnic Mexicans, destruction of homes and ranches, forced relocation, and mass, extralegal executions. Many from the Mexican-origin population fled across the Rio Grande to Mexico. Whereas the rebels killed dozens of Anglo farmers and temporarily drove many more—hundreds, perhaps thousands—from their homes and properties, American forces killed at least 300 according to the most conservative estimate, but some suggest that the death toll could have been as high as 5,000.[23]

In the decades following the Treaty of Guadalupe-Hidalgo, there was also widespread violence related to conflicts with indigenous peoples. The roots of the "Indian problem" predated the establishment of the postwar boundary. But the making of a line of control that restricted freedom of movement and the related settlement of the border region by settlers on both sides of the boundary (especially in the United States) furthered the socioeconomic marginalization of Native peoples and the dispossession of their lands. This in turn led to transboundary raids by indigenous groups, mostly originating in what was by then the United States, as they sought to overcome their deprivation, exacerbating tensions between Mexico and the United States in the process.[24] Article XI of the Treaty of Guadalupe Hidalgo required the United States, because it gained territory inhabited by "savage tribes," to prevent incursions into Mexico by Native peoples. Yet, for a number of years, the United States did not patrol its southern boundary. Its negligence not only facilitated many transboundary attacks by Native peoples against Mexico, but also those by U.S. filibusters intent on seizing control of Mexican territory. By the 1890s, however, conflict between the U.S. and Mexico over Indian raids and filibuster activity largely disappeared with the elimination or the relocation of "troublesome" indigenous groups to reservations, increasingly effective administrative and military control of the border region by both governments, and decreasing political and economic isolation of the borderlands from the centers of their respective countries.[25] Thus, by the early twentieth century (the period of the Mexican Revolution, roughly 1910–1920, when violence from the conflict spilled over into the United States, being an exception),[26] the U.S.-Mexico border region was largely pacified. But that was a far cry from establishing control over the transboundary movement of people and goods. This was a much longer process, one that continues to the present.

The ongoing nature of the process relates to the fact that effective immigration and boundary enforcement are practices of recent origin in human history, ones tied to the rise of the modern territorial state. Until the twentieth century, nation-state controls over the movement of peoples—with few exceptions—were very weak and often nonexistent around the globe.[27] There wasn't even general agreement that such controls were legitimate: a survey of international legal opinion in the period immediately preceding World War I, for example, found that there was no consensus that nation-states had a right to prevent nonnational citizens from entering their territory.[28] In that regard, one of the most striking aspects of the current boundary enforcement regime in the United States is how accepted and largely uncontroversial it is within American society. (One could make the same observation about boundary and immigration enforcement throughout the world, especially in high-income countries.)

Relative to most parts of the world, the United States was a pioneer in establishing boundary and immigration enforcement. Yet, with the exception of the Alien Friends Act of 1798 which empowered the president to arrest and deport any foreigner regarded as "dangerous to the peace and safety of the United States," there was no federal legislation restricting immigration into the country until the 1870s.[29] From that time until the early twentieth century, Congress passed a whole host of laws barring the entry of non-U.S. citizens on the basis of qualitative characteristics such as race, national origin, physical and mental health, and political beliefs. Legislation in 1875, for example, excluded convicts and prostitutes, and an 1882 law barred "idiots, lunatics, convicts, and persons likely to become public charges." The year 1882 also marked the passing of the Chinese Exclusion Act, the first piece of legislation that restricted immigration on the basis of national origins. The next several decades saw a widening of such restrictions. In fact, it was not until 1952 that Congress passed legislation making persons from all "races" eligible for immigration and naturalization as citizens—for the first time since Congress had restricted citizenship to "free white persons" in 1790.[30]

Restrictions led to efforts to circumvent them and, thus, boundary and immigration enforcement, but it was slow in coming. The Chinese Exclusion Act presented the first significant challenge to U.S. authorities along the U.S-Mexico boundary. Until 1882, the Bureau of Immigration, established during the Civil War, functioned to *encourage* immigration from Europe and as a gatherer of statistics. Chinese exclusion, however, resulted in the bureau's receiving field operatives—called "Chinese Inspectors"—who worked out of ports of entry along the international boundary under the jurisdiction of the collectors of customs.[31] But the fact that the smuggling of Chinese migrants into the United States was a highly lucrative and well-organized business, combined with the porosity of the boundary, ensured that most Chinese migrants who wanted to enter the United States from Mexico without authorization surely did so.[32]

This also reflected just how small the boundary enforcement infrastructure was in the late 1800s and early 1900s. Controls were so minimal, in fact, that authorities maintained no records from 1886 to 1893.[33] The federal government concentrated its resources on immigration from Europe and on the divide with Canada rather than that with Mexico. Its efforts focused largely at official ports of entry such as Ellis Island near New York City. To the extent that the Mexican boundary was monitored, the focus was on Chinese and other non-

Mexican immigrants.[34] The relatively limited points (and methods) of entry into the United States as well as insufficient infrastructure and resources of the U.S. government led to little reliance on a boundary enforcement strategy. As a U.S. Customs official described in an undated report probably from 1902 or 1903, there were only three U.S. authorities on the entire California boundary. The writer went on to complain, "Except in the vicinity of Tia Juana [today known as San Ysidro] and Campo [thirty miles east of San Ysidro] . . . the entire boundary line is unguarded and open, presenting no barrier to free and unrestricted trade between the two countries."[35]

The number of customs and immigration officials increased thereafter, but boundary policing remained quite lax for the next few decades. Even though the Immigration Service began demanding passports of all who wanted to cross from Mexico into the United States in 1917 in the context of World War I, the requirement was often not enforced.[36] Moreover, the ability of U.S. authorities to patrol the boundary was still very limited. As of February 1918, for example, there were five immigrant inspectors stationed in Calexico, one in Campo, and four in "Tia Juana"—along with a small number of soldiers who assisted them.[37] As the supervising inspector of the Mexican Border District wrote about enforcement measures along the U.S.-Mexico boundary in general, "so long as the border is not adequately guarded, the restrictive measures employed at ports of entry simply tend to divert the illegal traffic to unguarded points, of which there are literally thousands."[38]

The disorder brought about by the Mexican Revolution played an important role in turning the boundary into an obstacle for Mexican migrants. Congress responded in part with the Immigration Act of 1917, which, while exempting Mexicans (until a new law in 1921), led to a formalization of immigration control procedures as well as to an increase in the number of U.S. authorities and immigration inspection sites along the boundary. The new practices applied to Mexican migrants attempting to cross the boundary included (depending on the assessment and dictates of the U.S. immigrant inspectors at official ports of entry) vaccination, bathing, and delousing. Medical experts hired by the Immigration Service designated the migrants as either "desirable" or "undesirable" based on their health.[39]

The implementation of a literacy test, mandated by the 1917 legislation, further complicated the process of crossing the boundary, as did the imposition of an $8 head tax for all immigrants. The addition in 1924 of an obligatory visa (for a $10 fee) for all immigrants only added to the financial burden of crossing the boundary.[40] Nevertheless, most unauthorized Mexican migrants still managed to enter the United States successfully. As of 1919, there were only 151 immigrant inspectors, who were responsible for more than two thousand miles of boundary and most of whom were obligated to remain at one of the twenty official ports of entry. At times, the Immigration Service had a total force of available mobile guards that numbered no more than sixty.[41] As the chief immigration inspector in El Paso remarked in about 1920, "practically any alien desirous of entering the United States and possessed of ordinary intelligence and persistence could readily find the means to do so without fear of detection."[42]

The outbreak of World War I had led the U.S. government to implement travel restrictions and to deploy troops along the boundary. Yet, the increased demands on boundary enforcement officials brought about by the war (including the inspection of all people crossing from the United States into Mexico) overwhelmed authorities. It was during this time that discussions to establish a permanent patrol force along the international divide began. They continued and intensified as unauthorized entries picked up quickly following the end of the war, especially in the face of large numbers of apprehensions of unauthorized European and Chinese immigrants

Nogales, Arizona, U.S.A. and Nogales, Sonora, Mexico. July 2006. U.S. boundary wall.

smuggled in from Canada, Mexico, and Cuba, and widespread fear that huge numbers of migrants from war-torn Europe might try to enter the United States extralegally. Such factors, combined with concerns about maintaining Anglo racial dominance, led to the imposition in 1921 of restrictions that limited the number of admissions of any one particular nationality to 3 percent of the group's population already in the United States as reflected by the 1910 census. Three years later, passage of the Johnson-Reed Act of 1924 required immigrants for the first time to obtain visas from U.S. consular officials abroad before traveling to the United States.[43] It was in this context of concerns about unauthorized migrants from China and war-torn Europe, fears of racial swamping by undesirable "aliens," and a preoccupation with matters of national security that the U.S. Border Patrol was born.

On May 28, 1924, Congress granted 1 million dollars for its establishment. It had an initial force of 450 officers assigned to the Mexican and Canadian borders as well as to the Florida and Gulf of Mexico coasts.[44] Through the 1920s and 1930s, the Border Patrol grew slowly.[45] During this time, roughly an equal number of agents worked in the Canadian and Mexican border regions. Until the repeal of Prohibition in 1933, the agency concentrated a significant amount of its resources to preventing the smuggling of alcohol into the United States. Following the repeal, it focused its efforts on preventing the entry of unauthorized crossings from Mexico.[46]

The year 1940 marked a turning point for the Border Patrol. The outbreak of World War II helped bring about fears that dangerous foreign agents would attempt to enter U.S. territory. In this context, Congress appropriated two million dollars to add 712 Border Patrol officers (allowing for an almost doubling of the force), 57 auxiliary personnel, and new equipment. Agents carried out many functions during the war, including guarding "enemy alien" detention camps as well as helping the U.S. military guard the Atlantic Coast against the potential entry of spies from the Axis powers.[47]

While the Border Patrol and the larger enforcement infrastructure grew, larger realities undermined the agency's stated mission. First and foremost, the length of the boundaries for which it was responsible limited its effectiveness, especially in the face of its relatively small size, the sophistication of smugglers, and the large numbers and sheer determination of migrants.[48] Furthermore, the Border Patrol had to contend with the intense transboundary social networks of the border region, many of which long preceded the establishment of the international boundary. In addition, farmers along the U.S. side of the divide actively encouraged Mexican workers to step across the line and work on their farms. According to an INS report in 1934, this was a practice difficult to stop, given the Border Patrol's insufficient numbers, and difficult to prosecute successfully because of the sympathy of juries to the needs of growers.[49]

Throughout most of the twentieth century, agricultural interests throughout the Southwest played a central role in producing and maintaining a yawning gap between official rhetoric championing strong boundary policing, and actual practice.[50] Thus, it not surprising that there was little serious political will among national political leaders, especially those from border states, to provide significant funding for boundary and immigration policing until relatively recently. In 1952 and 1954, for instance, a time at which many in Washington, D.C. were arguing that "illegal" migration from Mexico had reached a crisis point, many members of Congress from border states voted to cut monies appropriated to the Border Patrol. By 1954, the Border Patrol was only able to employ 200 agents at any one time.[51]

Relatively low resource levels continued during the 1960s and much of the 1970s. Although the number of apprehensions of unauthorized entrants rose almost fivefold during the 1960s, for example, the number of permanent INS positions remained constant. The Border Patrol's 1980 budget was only $77 million, less than that of the Baltimore police department and far less than half that of the Philadelphia police department.[52] Thus, while attempts by the federal government to control the entry and residence of migrants grew significantly over the first several decades of the twentieth century, these efforts were inconsistent and riddled with internal contradictions, especially in regards to unauthorized entrants from Mexico.

—✦—

It would be a mistake to thus conclude that what took place along the U.S.-Mexico boundary through most of the twentieth century was a mere show, or that immigration authorities were only pawns serving the interests of agribusiness more broadly. Instead, what all this illustrates is the deep ambivalence that American society had—and still has—about immigration, and specifically about migrants from "south of the border." It is also very much a manifestation of the competing pressures of a business elite that has generally been very desirous of relatively free migration and a wide swath of the population that has long generally favored strong migratory restrictions for multiple reasons, but most consistently and deeply owing to concerns about national identity—one very much tied to notions of race, ethnicity, and language. Whether a relatively "open door" approach to immigration has prevailed or a restrictionist one has always been a function of socioeconomic context and how political actors and institutions mobilize at particular times and places.

In the period between 1910 and 1929, for example, Mexican migrant workers were largely welcome in the Southwest. Many U.S. elites in fact praised what they saw as their industriousness and docility. But such affection quickly disappeared as Mexican workers became involved in militant unions and often participated in strikes, strikes that local authorities—in conjunction with the growers—frequently repressed with great violence.[53] By 1930, few members of the ruling classes still believed in the docility of Mexican workers. Labor militancy combined with perceptions of the politics associated with the Mexican Revolution led U.S. elites in general to see Mexican workers increasingly as a threat—often Communist-inspired. As one congressman (John Box of Texas) asserted in response to the 1928 cantaloupe workers strike in the Imperial Valley, "Mexico is by far the most Bolshevistic country in the Western Hemisphere."[54]

Such views and the context of the Great Depression of the 1930s facilitated Mexicans' becoming a convenient scapegoat for a variety of social ills, with organizations ranging from the American Federation of Labor to the American Legion and the Veterans of Foreign Wars leading the charge.[55] It was in such a climate that a forced repatriation of tens of thousands of Mexicans took place in the 1930s, often through methods that even a 1932 U.S. government commission characterized as "unconstitutional, tyrannic and oppressive."[56] According to one study, U.S. authorities forcibly expelled an estimated 415,000 Mexicans between 1929 and 1935, with another 85,000 leaving "voluntarily," usually under intense pressure from local authorities. Some estimates of the deportations run as high as one million, including tens of thousands of U.S. citizens of Mexican descent.[57] A significant effect of the mass deportations was to slow Mexican immigration to a negligible level. But it picked up again in 1942—in response to labor shortages brought about by the World War II. That year also marked the beginning of the Bracero Program.[58]

Many expected the program to reduce unauthorized migration from Mexico, but the opposite seems to have happened.[59] Large numbers of growers continued to prefer hiring "illegal" migrants as it was less cumbersome and less expensive than hiring braceros. Meanwhile, the INS actually encouraged the increase in extralegal migration through its own actions. In 1947, for example, a year when relatively few braceros were imported, the INS instituted a de facto legalization program for unauthorized migrants discovered working in agriculture, contracting them out to employers as braceros. This informal legalization program continued to be an integral part of the Bracero Program for several years.[60] This process (popularly known as "drying out the wetbacks") served to increase unsanctioned migration from Mexico as the news spread that the easiest manner to obtain a bracero contract was to enter the United States extralegally.[61]

In response to the growth in unauthorized migrant entries, numerous officials began to argue that such levels of uncontrolled migration could potentially present a threat to the stability of the agricultural economy and the larger society as well. The 1951 report of the President's Commission on Migratory Labor was the first to sound the alarm, blaming unauthorized migration for depressing wage rates in the Southwest and warning of its implications for public health and housing standards. Although growers and their congressional allies attacked the report, it helped to intensify critical attention on unsanctioned migration, and to link it to all sorts of social problems, including crime and the threat of Communist subversion. Organized labor also fanned the flames. Such critiques resonated with large segments of the public, especially given the severe recession of 1953–54, the Cold War and the prevailing anticommunism.[62] Some, while stressing the national security dimensions of the perceived crisis, also emphasized the law-and-order aspect. One INS official, for example, proclaimed the increasing number of extralegal entrants from Mexico to be "the greatest peacetime invasion ever complacently suffered by another country under open, flagrant, contemptuous violations of its laws."[63]

Although the Eisenhower administration was generally ambivalent in its response, growing pressure from Congress, segments of the public, and officials in border states led it to launch the offensively named "Operation Wetback" on June 9, 1954. The operation involved the massive roundup of suspected unauthorized migrants in the border region. According to the INS, the agency apprehended more than one million migrants during fiscal year 1954, most of the apprehensions taking place during the operation. By means of highly visible, geographically concentrated shows of force in particular locales and sensationalized media coverage, the INS was able to give the impression of being far more powerful than it was, thus causing,

San Diego, California, U.S.A. March 2001. Double-layered barrier with maquiladora on Mexican side. The Real ID Act of 2005 granted the U.S. Department of Homeland Security the right to waive all laws, including environmental regulations, in order to construct barriers and roads anywhere along the U.S.-Mexico boundary. The Secure Fence Act of 2006 authorized the construction of 700 miles of double-layered fencing.

reported the agency, "uncounted thousands" of unauthorized migrants to leave the country on their own. Although Operation Wetback resulted in a record number of deportations, the federal government compensated agricultural interests by greatly increasing the number of braceros admitted into the United States. In this regard, a key outcome of the operation was to increase state and grower control over migrant labor.[64] At the same time, the operation helped to quell critics of the agency, while countering its negative image within Congress and the society as a whole as inept and beholden to big agriculture.[65]

While the undertaking was significant in and of itself, it was also an important component of a much larger process. The combination of high-profile events such as the pacification of the borderlands in the last half of the nineteenth century, the slow building up of the boundary and its enforcement apparatus in the period beginning in 1882, and the mass deportations in the 1930s and Operation Wetback in 1954, all helped to make the U.S.-Mexico boundary "real." They not only gave substance to the actual territorial line by legitimizing and strengthening ports of entry and exit, fences and other physical demarcations, and patrols and inspections by a variety of law-enforcement bodies, but also by drawing on and furthering the social and legal divisions that empowered U.S. authorities to carry out all sorts of acts against migrants under the rubric of the law. As a result, U.S. efforts to control the boundary with Mexico and to regulate the people who crossed it became progressively uncontroversial and "normal" by the 1950s. Indeed, growing numbers of people began to expect and demand regulation of migration and the boundary, a manifestation of how profoundly the process had shaped the national geographical imagination. As such, the boundary increasingly helped to territorially and socially define and separate the United States and Mexico, Americans and Mexicans, and places and peoples from beyond. These highly significant developments laid the foundation for the "border war" that emerged in the 1970s.

―w―

Beginning in the late 1960s and early 1970s, there was growing public perception of the international boundary with Mexico as "out of control," as a dangerously porous line of defense against unprecedented numbers of unauthorized migrants entering the United States from Mexico. Prior to that time, the U.S.-Mexico boundary rarely received national-level attention. When it did—as around the time of Operation Wetback—it was fairly short-lived.

A number of factors dovetailed to precipitate the perception of an insufficiently secure boundary and a crisis of "illegal" migration, one associated mostly with Mexico. The advent of a Chicano civil rights movement in the late 1960s, whose most notable accomplishments took place in the border region, led many American elites to fear the rise in the U.S. Southwest of an "American Quebec"—a reference to the secessionist movement in the Canadian province.[66] The early- and mid-1970s saw the emergence of an energy crisis and an economic downturn in the United States that significantly impacted broad sectors of the U.S. population. Simultaneously, apprehensions of unauthorized migrants were rising rapidly (in part because of the ending of the Bracero Program, which led to the previously legal influx going underground), approaching the levels that preceded the implementation of Operation Wetback. In this context "illegal immigration" and "border control" emerged as topics of intense media interest about 1973. Indeed, all the major media, beginning in the 1970s, featured stories highlighting the putative problems associated with unauthorized immigration, and largely that from Mexico.[67] A variety of federal officials and national politicians, along with a compliant media, helped to construct the perception of a crisis and to stoke public fears.

The person heading the INS during most of the Ford administration (1974–77) was ex-Marine general Leonard Chapman, who had been appointed to that position in 1973 by President Richard Nixon. Chapman greatly contributed to the perception of a crisis through his outspokenness and effective use of the media platform afforded by his position.[68] But Chapman was hardly alone in bringing about a shift in public perception. President Gerald Ford, for instance, tried to blame the country's economic problems on unauthorized migrants, stating in 1976, "The main problem is how to get rid of those 6 to 8 million aliens who are interfering with our economic prosperity."[69]

Increasingly politicians and public officials began putting forth dire warnings of a security threat to the United States represented by unauthorized migration, often employing metaphors suggesting an invasion. William B. Saxbe, the U.S. attorney general under Ford, for example, called the presence of such migrants "a severe national crisis." Mentioning jobs, crime, and welfare costs, Saxbe called for the deportation of one million "illegal aliens" whom he described as mostly Mexicans.[70] Former CIA director William Colby stated that unauthorized Mexican migration was a greater future threat to the United States than the Soviet Union.[71] "The most obvious threat," Colby warned, "is the fact that . . . there are going to be 120 million Mexicans by the end of the century. . . . [The Border Patrol] will not have enough bullets to stop them."[72]

The press played a key role in legitimating the perception of a proverbial invasion from Mexico by uncritically recounting and providing a platform for INS allegations that unauthorized migrants were producers of poverty, crime, and joblessness.[73] In 1974, for instance, the *New York Times* reported INS Commissioner Chapman's claim before a congressional subcommittee that he could open up one million jobs "virtually overnight" for unemployed Americans.[74] Two years later, the *Reader's Digest* published an article by Chapman in which he claimed that "we could reduce our own unemployment dramatically— *as much as 50 percent*" if U.S. authorities "could locate and deport three to four million illegals who currently hold jobs in the United States, replacing them with citizens and legal residents."[75] Such characterizations and media activism, combined with activity within Congress and the White House, helped to give rise to an increasingly anti-immigrant public sentiment as evidenced by opinion polls. It was in this context that numerous federal officials, national politicians, and a variety of national organizations began agitating for increased resources for the INS and, especially, boundary policing in the 1970s.[76]

The Carter administration (1977–1981) continued the trend. Arguing that extralegal migrants "had breached [the] Nation's immigration laws, displaced many American citizens from jobs, and placed an increased financial burden on many state and local governments," President Jimmy Carter announced an immigration plan in mid-1977. It included a call to double the Border Patrol's size and to implement employer sanctions as well as a legalization program.[77] While Carter's initiative did not succeed, it, along with associated undertakings, helped lay the foundation for subsequent debate and legislation regarding immigration control, and the perception of an "illegal" migration and boundary crisis.

The single event that probably contributed the most to this crisis mentality, which was increasingly informing much of the public debate on issues of boundary policing and immigration, was the Mariel boatlift from Cuba that saw about 125,000 Cuban refugees arrive along the Miami coast in 1980.[78] Advocates of enhanced boundary policing and stricter immigration laws quickly seized upon the influx to support their positions.[79] This—combined with Cold War tensions that the Reagan administration and others manipulated to translate into perceived threats of terrorism emanating from Central America—led to a growing number of Americans seeing the country as under siege from without and the boundary as an insufficiently guarded line of protection.

These sociopsychological shifts had real-world effects, albeit gradual ones. During the second half of the Carter administration, the Border Patrol grew slightly—from 2,189 agents nationwide in 1978 to 2,474 in 1980—while, along the boundary, there was a significant upgrading of equipment, ranging from increased construction of fences to the deployment of helicopters and improved ground sensors.[80] The growth intensified much more during Ronald Reagan's two terms in office (1981–89), with the former actor often justifying the expansion on the basis of national security grounds.[81] During that time, congressional funding for the INS increased 130 percent and staff positions grew 41 percent. U.S. officials rationalized much of the increase on the grounds of fighting drug trafficking during Reagan's second term, although much of the increase helped immigration enforcement as well.[82] In the context of the Reagan administration's growing "war on drugs," the Border Patrol became increasingly preoccupied with drug interdiction. Indeed, the so-called war waged by Reagan and his successor in the White House, George H. W. Bush, was one of the most significant factors that fueled the boundary build-up, which contrasted with a previous, almost exclusive focus on unauthorized migration. Although the Drug Enforcement Agency at the time estimated that that about 85 percent of illegal drugs entering the United States arrived through official ports of entry (land, sea, or air), the Reagan-Bush drug war focused its efforts largely on the boundary in between the official ports of entry. In doing so, the two administrations significantly helped to associate boundary enforcement with criminal activity.[83]

While intensified boundary policing to interdict drugs and unauthorized migrants had taken place on numerous occasions in the past, what marked the build-up beginning in the second half of the Carter administration was its sustained nature. Rather than being a merely temporary development, that phase of boundary militarization marked a significant hardening of the U.S.-Mexico divide and a dramatic upsurge in collective consciousness about its importance and necessity.[84] At the same time, it was a manifestation of the intensification of another process begun in the mid-1800s, namely, the pacification of the border region. Yet, while the 1970s marked the beginning of deep and sustained concern about migration across the United-States-Mexico boundary, the 1990s saw the emergence of historically unprecedented levels of concern about unsanctioned migration and, associated with that, an "out of control" southern divide.

This boundary-making process, in terms of its ideological and practical roots and manifestations, had long involved both national and local players. But, beginning in the 1970s, the importance of actors in the border region in shaping the national debate increased dramatically. In some ways, areas in the border region, reflective of its heightened demographic and political-economic weight, became the proverbial tail that wagged the (national) dog. Nowhere was this more true than in California in the early 1990s, most notably in the southern part of the state, especially traditionally, white, middle-class areas of greater Los Angeles and San Diego.[85]

This occurred for a number of reasons. In the late 1980s and early 1990s, an estimated 400,000 people a year were migrating (legally and extralegally) to California.[86] At the same time, California was experiencing a serious recession (one that hit the southern part of the state especially hard), the breakdown of local government, a widening gap between rich and poor, and a massive racial recomposition. California was one of the whitest states in the United States in 1960; by the early 1990s, it was the most racially and ethnically diverse.[87] All of these

Douglas, Arizona, U.S.A. June 2004. Bottom photo: Monitoring migrant crossings from the Douglas Border Patrol station.

From the U.S. Customs and Border Protection Web site:

> "The priority mission of the Border Patrol is preventing terrorists and terrorists [*sic*] weapons, including weapons of mass destruction, from entering the United States." (http://www.cbp.gov/xp/cgov/border_security/border_patrol/)

developments dovetailed neatly with California's history of racism and anti-immigrant sentiment and provided ample fuel for demagogic politicians and a host of anti-immigrant groups, making California the national leader in the 1990s in raising the anti-immigration banner, especially in relation to the U.S.-Mexico boundary.

A combination of grassroots, prorestrictionist groups and politicians from southern California played the lead role in advocating the boundary build-up. California Governor Pete Wilson was especially key. In 1991, he blamed both legal and extralegal migrants for much of the state's budget crisis. Soon Wilson went national with his anti-immigration campaign, castigating the federal government for failing to control the southern boundary and for failing to appropriate billions of dollars promised by the Reagan administration to border states to pay for health, education, and welfare services to immigrants—a stance that resonated strongly with much of the California electorate.

Many Republicans—both in Sacramento, the state capital, and in Washington, D.C.—soon joined Wilson's efforts to increase immigration enforcement and restriction, with a focus primarily on unauthorized migration from Mexico. And various national-level, anti-immigration organizations—such as the Washington, D.C.–based Federation for American Immigration Reform (FAIR)—added fuel to the fire.

It was out of these efforts that California's Proposition 187 emerged. Also known as the "Save Our State" (SOS) initiative, Proposition 187 was a 1994 state ballot measure that sought to deny public education (from elementary to post-secondary levels), public social services, and public health-care services (with the exception of emergencies) to unauthorized migrants. Numerous politicians—most famously, Pete Wilson whose reelection bid for governor was flagging until he embraced 187—rode the ballot measure to electoral success. The largely white California electorate, for its part, also embraced 187 enthusiastically, passing it by an almost 3-2 margin.

Although restrictionist sentiment was most intense in California, it reached historic highs throughout the country. Part of this was due to the perceived failure of the 1986 Immigration Reform and Control Act (IRCA) to bring about a decrease in extralegal migration. IRCA made it illegal for employers to *knowingly* hire unauthorized migrant workers and required them to make a good-faith effort to attest to the immigration status of their employees; it also resulted in the legalization of upward of 3 million unauthorized migrants—the vast majority of whom were Mexican—living and working in the United States. Although IRCA did lead to a rapid decline in Border Patrol apprehensions (largely owing to the legalization program), apprehensions along the southern boundary, especially the California section through which most unauthorized migrants passed at the time, quickly began to rise again in 1989.[88] In addition, the earlier pro-immigration consensus was breaking down among both liberal and conservative elites. Most importantly, efforts by conservatives and the Republican Party over the years had provided fertile ideological ground for the issues of unauthorized immigration and boundary enforcement by the early 1990s.[89] That 1992 was a federal election year only increased the rising tide of anti-immigration efforts on the part of national politicians and organizations.

A number of contextual factors and high-profile events in early 1993 helped to increase the associated pressure, by quickly bringing migration and the southern boundary to the fore of national consciousness. These included the following: fears of a huge influx of Haitian refugees; a persistent economic recession; the bombing of the World Trade Center by suspected unauthorized immigrants; and the assassination of two Central Intelligence Agency employees in Vir ginia by an unauthorized immigrant from Pakistan.[90] But most important in helping to create the popular image of the United States under invasion from foreign hordes was the discovery off U.S. shores of ships carrying unauthorized Chinese migrants, especially the *Golden Venture* and its cargo of 286 Chinese which ran aground in the waters of New York City on June 6, 1993. While such events had nothing to do with unauthorized immigration from Mexico, they significantly contributed to a growing perception of a country under siege from without and to anti-immigration sentiment of historic highs on the national level.[91] Perceiving this general mood, politicians rushed to take a tough stance on boundary enforcement and unauthorized migration—especially in California.

Although boundary enforcement was a very low priority for the Clinton administration when it took office in 1993, it could not ignore the sentiment in California given the state's electoral importance—both in terms of the 1994 congressional elections and Clinton's reelection bid in 1996. Moreover, congressional Republicans had begun to increase their anti-immigration rhetoric, betting their party stood to gain most from the voting public that perceived immigration as a significant threat. This strategy pressured the Clinton administration and the Democrats to engage the issue more as the midterm elections of 1994 approached.

The White House and its Democratic allies were greatly worried about the political fallout if the public were to perceive that they were not responding adequately to these developments. But rather than challenge the growing restrictionist sentiment and the underlying assumptions, the Democratic leadership embraced them while trying to distinguish themselves from the Republicans such as Pete Wilson by opposing Proposition 187, and championing other solutions to the putative problems of immigration and boundary control. As such, many Democratic Party supporters and politicians, as well as Clinton appointees, urged the administration to get out in front of efforts to restrict unauthorized migration to prevent the passage of Republican proposals even more drastic than those proposed at the time.[92] It was in this context that the Clinton administration soon announced high-profile plans to enhance control of the boundary and to steal the Republican political thunder in the process. On October 1, 1994, it launched Operation Gatekeeper in southern California, which would become the centerpiece of a larger national strategy, and began facilitating the significant infusion of resources that resulted in the dramatic changes in the U.S.-Mexico boundary and immigration enforcement apparatus that we see today.[93]

—〜〜—

The effects of such operations—and boundary and immigration policing more broadly—have always been uneven, and less than that desired by their most vociferous advocates. In the case of the massive roundups and deportations associated with Operation Wetback in 1954, for example, an account of enforcement in Calexico-Mexicali from two years later characterized restrictions at the ports of entry as "trifling": "Any citizen of United States [*sic*] enters Mexico at will without passport or papers," it read. "Any Mexican citizen of good character may obtain an American Visitors Card, good any time."[94]

More than anything else, what such a description captures is the inherently discriminatory nature of boundary regulation. Mexicans of "bad" character—presumably a very broad category that includes unauthorized migrant laborers—certainly had long faced restrictions that were more than "trifling." Efforts like Operation Wetback and the steady growth of the enforcement apparatus along the country's perimeter markedly helped to fortify its boundaries and had powerful effects on the lives of many migrants. Yet overall they had little impact on the number of entries—authorized and unauthorized—into the United States. In the case of the period from 1880 to World War I, for example, U.S. immigration authorities excluded only one percent of the 25 million European migrants who arrived in the United States—this despite a growing list of categories that permitted exclusion.[95]

Nonetheless, boundary and immigration enforcement significantly helped to shape the migrants themselves and the national socio-political-economic fabric. All migrants passing through official ports of entry in the late 1800s and early 1900s, for instance, were inspected—for diseases and defects, among other things. By determining who was "fit" to enter and join the country's rapidly expanding industrial workforce, U.S. authorities were not only serving the interests of capital, but more importantly were defining what it meant to be "American," and who belonged and who did not. In this regard, asserts historian Amy Fairchild, migrant regulation was and is part of a process of inclusion, just as it was one of exclusion.[96]

The U.S. Public Health Service's *Manual for the Physical Inspection of Aliens* (1917) provides insight as to what U.S. government officials saw as "American" and its antithesis. Among the classes of people to be blocked from entering the country that the publication listed were the following: imbeciles, idiots, feeble-minded persons, persons of constitutional psychopathic inferiority—a category that included pathological liars and persons with abnormal sexual instincts (homosexuals)—vagrants, physical defectives, chronic alcoholics, polygamists, anarchists, persons afflicted with loathsome or dangerous diseases, prostitutes, contract laborers, and all aliens over 16 years old who could not read.[97]

The exclusion of such undesirables was stronger at some locations than others. And, as such, migrants attempting to pass through "harder" ports of entry were typically cast as more alien than those coming through, say, Ellis Island. Not surprisingly, it was the U.S.-Mexico boundary that was often the point of greatest concern among U.S. authorities. As the commissioner general of immigration stated in 1906, "the very worst elements of the foreigners enter by that route."[98] Consequently, migrants of Mexican and Latin American origin (along with those from Africa and China) deemed as diseased by U.S. authorities, for instance, were typically far more likely to be deported than western Europeans of similarly inadequate health.[99] As such, health-related boundary policing helped to racialize particular groups as well as to make the boundary more of an obstacle.

This was true for those admitted (the vast majority of would-be entrants) as well. In El Paso in 1917 alone, 127,173 Mexicans were bathed and deloused at the bridge that joined the United States with Ciudad Juárez.[100] There, all immigrants from the Mexican interior, and those whom U.S. officials deemed "second-class" residents of Juarez, had to, according to historian David Romo, "strip completely, turn in their clothes to be sterilized in a steam dryer and fumigated with hydrocyanic acid, and stand naked before a Customs inspector who would check his or her 'hairy parts'—scalp, armpits, chest, genital area — for lice. Those found to have lice would be required to shave their heads and body hair with clippers and apply a mix of kerosene and vinegar on his body."[101] Such measures were supposedly in response to the threat of typhus from Mexico. Yet, even though the typhus scare soon disappeared, delousings and sprayings continued in many U.S. border towns until the late 1950s. The fumigants employed included Zyklon B—which seems to have inspired the Nazis to use the gas in the death chambers of their concentration camps, albeit at much higher dosages, applying it directly on people, rather than on clothing as U.S. officials did—and DDT.[102]

The perceived need for security was informed not only by public-health concerns, but also (among other factors) notions of racial purity and fears of middle-class "race suicide," sentiments that were especially powerful in the early 1900s, a time when eugenics, or racial science, was ascendant. (One cannot divorce the Border Patrol's founding in 1924 from an era when eugenics was the rage. In this regard, its founding was about, among other things, maintaining Anglo racial domination.)[103]

What all this illustrates, as writer and photographer David Bacon has observed about the contemporary period, is that the effect of U.S. immigration enforcement is not so much to stop migration, but to define the status of people—as subordinate—once they have arrived. As such, migrants that succeed in crossing have to deal with the indignities and insecurity associated with being "aliens," "illegals," or both.[104]

Underlying the subordination has always been various ideological characterizations that serve to justify the lesser status imposed on migrants. From the national security threat attached to undesirable migrants in the aftermath of the American Revolutionary War, to the moral corrosion that restrictionist legislation in the late 1800s and early 1900s associated with migrants, to the focus on Mexican women as a demographic threat because of their supposed hyperfertility and mythical heavy reliance on social services, to the criminal status increasingly assigned to unauthorized migrants by virtue of their very "illegal" presence in the United States, large numbers of non-U.S. nationals within U.S. territory have long been characterized in unflattering and, often, debilitating ways.[105] The roots of American nativism go back to the English colonial period. In a 1753 letter, for example, Benjamin Franklin wrote of German immigrants, "Few of their children in the country learn English. . . . The signs in our streets have inscriptions in both languages. . . . Unless the stream of their importation could be turned they will soon so outnumber us that all the advantages we have will not be able to preserve our language, and even our government will become precarious." Franklin

Tohono O'odham Nation. June 2004. Mike Wilson of Humane Borders provides water for migrants crossing through this desert area near Sells, Arizona. Seventy-five miles of boundary cuts through the Tohono O'odham Nation's traditional territory (from Phoenix, Arizona, to Hermosillo, Sonora). The U.S. enforcement strategy has created many hardships for the Tohono O'odham.*

----

called them "the most stupid of their nation."[106] Thus, while there is merit to the contention that the United States is a nation of immigrants, it is also the case that anti-immigrant sentiment is as American as apple pie.[107]

* One of the hardships created for Tohono O'odham is restrictions on the right to travel within their own lands. U.S. authorities only allow boundary crossings at official ports of entry (none of which are within the reservation). Moreover, many Tohono O'odham, having been born at home, do not have birth records, and thus have difficulty establishing their citizenship. This makes many on the U.S. side subject to arrest and deportation. For those who live on the Mexican side, lack of paperwork results in the inability to get a passport or a visa. The Nation's only health clinic is in Sells, north of the boundary. Many are no longer able to participate in religious ceremonies if held on the other side of the boundary from which they reside. (Castillo and Cowan 2001; Ellingwood 2004)

Although unauthorized migrants have more often than not received the brunt of opprobrium, it is the larger category of "undesirables" that is of greater significance, a category that includes not only "illegals," but also permanent residents and, at times, citizens, ones who are internal "minorities" deemed as threatening. As such, immigration restrictionist and nativist movements more broadly are first and foremost about defining what it means to be "American"—a concept that has historically been tied to white, English-speaking individuals.

This is not to say that the political-territorial cleansing process that immigration control entails has been exclusively a race-based one. Various restrictions have targeted groups on bases that cannot be reduced to "race" or national origins. In 1919–21, for example, the so-called Palmer Raids resulted in the deportation of hundreds of political "radicals" to Europe. And laws barring the entry into the United States of gay and lesbian "aliens" were in place until 1990.[108] But it has been the poor, nonwhite, largely peoples of so-called third-world origin that have been most consistently the objects of scrutiny, and the targets for deportation, detention, and other forms of control and exclusion. This is especially the case in the post-9/11 era when fears of terrorism are associated with people of color, particularly those born abroad or whose families are relatively recent arrivals to the United States.[109]

—◈—

By June 1998 when Julio César Gallegos arrived in Tijuana and tried to cross into the United States, this regime of control and exclusion along the U.S-Mexico border had reached unprecedented heights. Almost four years after the Clinton administration had begun to intensify boundary enforcement, promising to restore to the border region the rule of law—something that had never existed—the number of Border Patrol agents had grown dramatically. From 4,200 in Fiscal Year (FY) 1994, it had risen to almost 8,000 in FY 1998. In southern California alone, the number of Border Patrol agents grew from 980 to 2,264 agents during that period, along with a significant increase in the amount of boundary fencing and walls, underground sensors, and infrared scopes.

All this was occurring at a time of unparalleled levels of trans-boundary flows of goods and people—an increase which was greatly facilitated by the implementation of the North American Free Trade Agreement (NAFTA) in 1994. Indeed, NAFTA's anticipated consequences led INS commissioner Doris Meissner to state before Congress in November 1993, "Responding to the likely short-to-medium-term impacts of NAFTA will require strengthening our enforcement efforts along the border."[110] In other words, the liberalization of Mexico's economy would increase migratory pressures among those displaced in the name of economic efficiency, which in turn would require an increase in boundary policing. While this is only one of many factors that help to explain the rise of the boundary build-up, it demonstrates how in some regards "opening" and "closing" the boundary complement one another. At the same time, to the extent that the liberalization of the boundary has allowed for easier movement into the United States for the relatively elite in Mexico and beyond, while the simultaneous growth in restrictionism has made international mobility markedly more difficult for people on the socioeconomic margins of Mexico and elsewhere, they illustrate the two-tiered system of humanity inherent in a political-economic era many describe as neoliberal.[111]

Julio could have avoided all this had he been able to regularize his status in the United States. Legally, he was eligible to do so because of his marriage to Jackie. Financially, matters were more difficult. After getting married in 1995, Jackie and Julio consulted an immigration lawyer about fixing his status only to find out that it would cost him about $1,600 in fines (for being in the country without authorization) and filing fees. In addition, he would need to return to Mexico to file the request for a change in his immigration status. This represented an exorbitant cost for the newlyweds. That, combined with the fact that Julio had no plans to leave the United States, led them to decide to wait until 1998 to take care of matters. But before Julio and Jackie had saved sufficient funds to cover the costs of regularizing his immigration status—that year's federal tax refund would have given them enough—Julio had to go back to his hometown in Mexico to take care of some pressing family matters. That was in January 1998.

While in Mexico, Julio called Jackie regularly. He would often ask her to play family videos so that their son, Julio Jr., would not forget him. After spending six months in Mexico, he was especially eager to return to Los Angeles because Jackie was expecting another baby. As such, he tried to cross in the Tijuana-San Diego area in June of that year. But matters along the boundary had changed tremendously since the early 1990s when it was relatively easy to cross clandestinely. The Border Patrol apprehended Julio on four or five separate occasions in the area of San Diego. On his last attempt to cross there, someone robbed him.

Jackie spoke to him shortly thereafter on Father's Day—June 21, 1998. Julio told her that he was depressed because of the difficulties he was having in getting across the line and because he wasn't with his family. But he also expressed joy that he would soon be a father again as Jackie was six months pregnant at the time.

About one week later, Julio was still in Tijuana. A half sister of his living in Los Angeles, Maria del Refugio (also known as "Cuca"), spoke to him by phone. According to Jackie, Julio seemed desperate and told Cuca that he and the rest of his traveling companions were going to find a new *coyote*, and were going to try to cross near Mexicali. Cuca told him not to do so, that it was very dangerous, and that he could die trying to cross there. Julio agreed. Nonetheless, Julio, his 18-year-old niece, the *coyotes*, and some other migrants, went east to the desert and crossed into California near Calexico/Mexicali soon afterward.

Until the mid-1990s, crossing the boundary surreptitiously in the Imperial Valley was relatively easy. As one newspaper account explained, "For years, Calexico and Mexicali seemed like one city. The chain-link fence between the two was so flimsy that people would pull it aside and walk into the United States. Agents were often nowhere to be seen, and immigrants could easily cross the border and hop on buses or take taxis north out of the city."[112] But with Operation Gatekeeper—and especially with its 1997 expansion eastward from the San Diego Sector to the El Centro Sector, which covers the Valley—matters for unauthorized migrants in the area became much more difficult.

Showing how little they appreciated the resolve of migrants and the strength of factors driving migration, U.S. officials had predicted that the "territorial denial" strategies embodied by Operation Gatekeeper and similar operations in the Southwest would discourage many migrants from crossing into more urbanized zones. The concerted operations, they promised, would push migrants into mountain and desert areas where they would make a rational cost-benefit analysis in the face of adverse conditions and decide to give up and return home. As Julio and countless others have illustrated, however, it is an assumption with little basis in fact, one with often deadly consequences.

It is thought that Julio and his group crossed into the Imperial Valley from Mexico on June 30, but it is not known for certain. As the days and weeks passed after the last communication between him and the members of his extended family, they became extremely worried. Some of them went to Tijuana and elsewhere in Baja California

Norte to post photos and talk to Mexican officials to see if they could learn anything.[113] His father traveled from central Mexico to Los Angeles to find out what had happened, carrying Julio's best boots as his youngest son had asked him to bring them to him on his next visit.

Jackie became deeply depressed, desperate, and confused. A neighbor told her that she had recently seen Julio nearby, leaving Jackie to wonder if he had actually returned to Los Angeles and had decided not to rejoin his family. Around the same time, the Mexican Consulate in Calexico called her to say that they had information that Julio had returned to Zacatecas. A few days later, Julio Jr. began pointing at trees outside their home saying, "*Mira*, Daddy"—"Look, Daddy." When Jackie would approach him and ask where his father was, he'd say that he had run away from the tree just before Jackie had gotten there.

Tijuana, Baja California Norte, Mexico. September 2005. Alex had lived in Los Angeles for many years, and had been recently deported, leaving behind his partner and their young daughter.

On Thursday, August 13, 1998, the Mexican Consulate in Calexico called her again and told her that authorities had found seven or eight bodies in the desert. Jackie asked if they had found a young woman with the group. When the man from the consulate said "no," Jackie thought that it could not have been Julio's group, because her husband was traveling with his niece. Later, however, the consulate called back and told Jackie that there was indeed a young woman with the group.

Jackie went to work the next day. During lunch, she went to a nearby Catholic church and prayed. She called her mother, with whom she lived, several times to see if she had received any further news, but she told Jackie that she had not—even though she had already received confirmation from the consulate that one of the bodies was that of Julio.

When Jackie retuned home that night, her mother was sobbing; a neighbor was there with her. Jackie went into the kitchen and picked up Julio Jr. and just cried. She says that she did not talk all weekend. A lot of people came by her apartment to offer their condolences, but she has no recollection of their visits.

Julio's body arrived at the funeral home the next Monday. Jackie insisted on seeing the body, but the funeral home people refused her request as it was too decomposed. They did give her a small plastic bag from the Imperial Valley coroner's office, however, with the belongings found on him. It included a pay stub, toothbrush, wallet, and a baby photo of Julio Jr.

—⁓—

Ten years after Julio's death, the boundary and immigration enforcement apparatus is substantially bigger. In the El Centro Sector, for instance, there were about 800 Border Patrol agents in 2007—a quadrupling since 1994—and another 300 National Guard troops, along with seven miles of walls and fences made of mesh and steel bars, running east and west of the Calexico port of entry. Nationally, the Border Patrol had almost 15,000 agents in 2007—more than three times the amount the agency had in 1994.

Yet, despite such massive growth, unauthorized migrants continue to enter the United States via its southern boundary:[114] research undertaken in 2005 found that while it is much more difficult to cross now than in the early 1990s (about one-third get caught on any given trip) and that, as a result *some* in Mexico stay at home rather than even try, it also established that 92 to 97 percent of Mexican migrants continue to try to cross until they succeed, and that there has been no significant impact on the propensity of would-be migrants to attempt the journey.[115] This is not to suggest that further intensification of enforcement could not have a significant impact on the number of unauthorized entrants. (Plans are afoot to double the number of agents over the next decade and to build hundreds of miles of additional walls, fences, and vehicle barriers.) Indeed, in certain locales where enforcement personnel and infrastructure are concentrated, there has been a marked decline in unsanctioned crossings.[116] But given the depth and scale of the transboundary ties, the power of the forces driving migration, and the resolve and resourcefulness of migrants, it is pure fantasy to think that U.S. authorities can fully "secure" and regulate the boundary.[117]

While the dramatic increase in enforcement has not significantly reduced unauthorized crossings, it has diverted many billions of dollars from addressing pressing human needs. Moreover, it has led to migrants—authorized and unauthorized—present in the United States experiencing more harassment by police and immigration officials who employ racial and national-origin profiling and to communities in the border region living under constant surveillance and a heavily militarized police presence. It has also brought about a huge increase in detentions, including of children with their parents, imprisonment, and a massive growth in deportations—not only of so-called illegals but of permanent residents (some of whom have lived in the country for decades or since they were young children) who have been stripped of their right to be in the United States, often due to very minor legal infractions.[118] Even U.S. citizens are still sometimes mistakenly caught up in the growing deportation dragnet.[119] But even without such errors, the deportations profoundly impact U.S. nationals. Given the mixed-status nature of most migrant households—about 85 percent of migrant families (those with at least one noncitizen parent) are mixed status in that at least one child is a U.S. citizen[120]—an almost inevitable effect of deportations is to divide families.[121]

And for unauthorized migrants who manage to stay, the ongoing boundary build-up and growing repression have the effect of making it less likely that they will return to their country of origin, and drives them further into the shadows for fear of being caught by law enforcement officials.[122] At work, the growing enforcement web has the effect of "disciplining" labor by decreasing the likelihood that employees without proper papers will challenge substandard working conditions for fear of arrest and deportation. Such fear is well founded: according to one study, 52 percent of companies where union drives are taking place threaten to call U.S. immigration authorities if the organizing campaign involves unauthorized migrants.[123]

—⁓—

The growing policing and incarceration of migrants reflect, in numerous ways, sharpening divides between "legals" and illegals," and citizens and noncitizens.[124] They also reflect a momentous shift in the ideological and material weight of the U.S.-Mexico boundary.

From the time of the U.S.-Mexico War to the present, the line between the two countries has evolved from a mere line on a map, to a powerful divide and associated set of practices of inclusion and exclusion. The strength of this shift demonstrates the perception, and championing by many, of a neat, clear division between the United States and Mexico. This view denies the inherent messiness of social relations that defy national boundaries, and the strong, vibrant connections between places like the United States and Mexico—and the locations within. Those defending ever-greater levels of restriction along the boundary seek to limit these ties, or, at the very least, to selectively keep them at bay.

Migration is only one manifestation of such links, but it is also among the most controversial. While many pretend that it can be understood in a national vacuum—by asserting, for example, that it is exclusively Mexico's "fault" that many of its citizens migrate to the United States—it is and always has been an internationally driven phenomenon and, in the case of the United States and Mexico, very much a binational affair, one that involves dynamic ties between seemingly distant locales that are socially quite close. Such ties, ones between Julio's place of birth in Mexico and Jackie's hometown of Los Angeles, California, and ones significantly influenced by the very presence of the U.S.-Mexico boundary and its associated practices of social control were what brought him to the border region in the summer of 1998. And it was the nature of these ties that led to his untimely demise.

**Juchipila,
Zacatecas, Mexico.
January 2002.**

FOUR **JUCHIPILA, MEXUSA**

JULIO CÉSAR GALLEGOS WAS BORN on September 14, 1974, in Juchipila (hoo-chee-PEE-la), a town today with a population of about 9,400 people. It is a place that has many of the features one would find in numerous small towns in the U.S. Southwest. Cowboy and baseball hats are the headwear of choice for men and boys. For women and girls, the clothing styles are similar to those that one sees on many streets in southern California. Walking along the town's streets one hears a lot of Spanish, but also, on occasion, some English. Pickup trucks and, among the more prosperous, SUVs are popular. And a smattering of the vehicles have small American flags attached to their antennas. Its population is, in many ways, far more representative of the geographical diversity of the United States than one would expect to find in any U.S. town of a similar size. License plates from states like Oregon, Georgia, New Jersey, Nevada, and, in greatest number, California, adorn local vehicles.

In late January 2002 when I first visited there, the town's annual fair featured a rodeo, complete with bull riding and young cowgirls doing trick riding. Several months after the 9/11 terror attacks in New York City and Washington, D.C., the fiesta included a public lecture on anthrax and biological warfare.

The high point of the fair was when they crowned the town's queen and her court of princesses, after which there was a parade. Leading the parade were four pickups and SUVs; on the hood of each was a member of the royal beauty court. The last of the princesses sat on the hood of a big black truck with a Texas license plate. On the back windshield was a bumper sticker that said, "Proud to be American."

None of this seemingly mundane phenomena would be noteworthy were Juchipila not located in the state of Zacatecas in central Mexico. Mirroring the migratory nature of the state as a whole, it is estimated that the number of Juchipilans living in the United States exceeds the population of Juchipila. They are scattered all over the United States, with the largest number—perhaps even the majority— living in and around Los Angeles.

Juchipila—while as a locale is situated firmly within Mexico—is a

Juchipila, Zacatecas, Mexico. January 2002. One of the princesses of the annual town fiesta.

transnational place. It transcends the U.S.-Mexico boundary, and its native daughters and sons frequently travel back and forth across the divide. It is transnational to the extent the Juchipilans living in the United States help to reproduce Mexico as a nation-state. Its offspring abroad live in a manner that dynamically connects Juchipila to places, people, and processes in myriad locales throughout the United States. In this regard, Juchipila is also more than transnational: it is translocal in that the relationships that embody the town—materially and ideologically—involve place-to-place (and thus people-to-people) ties of an everyday nature.[1]

But the parts of "Juchipila" on the U.S. side of the boundary—places like Los Angeles, San Jose, Chino, and Sacramento in California, Elko in Nevada, Wendover in Utah, Houston and Galveston in Texas, and Riverdale in Georgia[2]—offer far greater levels of economic opportunity and security than those on the Mexican side. It is to a highly significant degree for this reason that crossing of the boundary for Juchipilans has become such a rite of passage. Yet, while the ties between the two are intense, they also reflect an uneven distribution of power and resources, as part of a larger relationship of inequality between Mexico and the United States. As such, one should avoid romanticizing Juchipila writ large—as a social space that transcends the U.S.-Mexico boundary, that effectively erases the divide. The boundary is very much present—in both Juchipila, Mexico and "Juchipila," USA—and thus powerfully informs the life-and-death circumstances of Juchipila's daughters and sons on whatever side of the line they find themselves. Indeed, the case of Juchipila—as with all such places so tied into international migration between the "first" and "third" worlds—illustrates that the international boundaries that divide and bring them together reflect and reproduce processes of inclusion and exclusion that are not limited to the site of the actual line, but ones that play out in places like Los

Angeles and inform their links with elsewhere. In this regard, Los Angeles, to where Julio migrated in 1993, in addition to being a center of dynamic growth and creative development, has always been a city that embodies the processes related to the very making of the U.S.-Mexico boundary—ones involving conquest, dispossession, subordination, domination, and nationalization. There, they play out in ways at least as intense, profound, and pervasive as anywhere else in the borderlands, making Los Angeles in many ways very much an American place, one where Mexicans as a whole, and especially those who are "illegal," are second-class citizens. There, in Juchipila, and in the links between them, the U.S.-Mexico boundary and its associated injustices loom large.

It is in this transnational space of Juchipila and specific places within—ones neither simply American nor Mexican—where Julio and his extended family lived their lives. These places, their particular histories, and the nature of their ties, divisions, inclusions, and exclusions help shape the lives, as well as the deaths, of all those connected to them. They also help shed light on the everyday workings of the U.S.-Mexico boundary and the larger set of dynamics that underlie it and that it helps to reproduce.

Juchipila lies in the southern end of Zacatecas, a region of canyons. It is the name of a *municipio* (the Mexican equivalent of a county), a town that serves as the municipio's seat of government,[3] and the larger canyon in which it is situated.

Juchipila was a political center for the indigenous population of the area, the original (pre-Spanish) name of which is Xochipillan (a moniker derived from Xochipilli, the Aztec god of love, games, dance, flowers, maize, and song). In 1530, the Spanish military attacked and occupied part of the area's indigenous kingdom. The Spanish conquered Juchipila in the mid-sixteenth century, the battle of Mixtón in 1542 marking the final major occurrence of violent resistance to Spain's empire in the area. The Spanish sent many of the indigenous survivors to other parts of what was to become Mexico as part of a strategy of lessening the likelihood of future rebellions. Those that remained clustered themselves in the town of Juchipila. Because of the armed conflict and epidemics brought about by the Spanish presence, the indigenous population of the tribute area of Juchipila was only 120 individuals by the end of the 1700s. But as the area's non-indigenous population grew owing to in-migration, the communities there gradually became "Mexican" and lost their indigenous character.[4]

Throughout the colonial period, Juchipila was the region's administrative hub. Following Mexican independence (1821), the town was also the site of many military battles during the periods of conflict involving those advocating a centralized Mexican nation-state and those championing a decentralized, federal form of government in the early decades of the country's independence and, later, in the upheavals associated with the Mexican Revolution in the first three decades of the twentieth century.[5]

The famous 1915 novel *Los de abajo* or *The Underdogs*, by Mariano Azuela, enshrines Juchipila as an important site of the Mexican Revolution. (Azuela, who served as a doctor in the army of Pancho Villa, eventually became disenchanted with the struggle. In addition to being outraged by the scale and depth of the bloodletting and destruction, he came to perceive the Revolution as ultimately betraying the country's underprivileged. While he saw the Revolution correcting some significant injustices, he also decried its hijacking by self-serving and unprincipled elites who had interests and goals contrary to those of the country's poor majority.)[6] Late in the novel, antigovernment forces march toward Juchipila, which, writes Azuela, "rose in the distance, white, bathed in sunlight, shining in the midst of a thick forest at the foot of a proud, lofty mountain, pleated like a turban." But as they enter the town's environs, the soldiers realize they have come upon a site of terrible violence as they see crosses along their path and on what remain of the walls of the town's buildings. These, the reader learns, are "traces of the first blood shed by the revolutionists of 1910, murdered by the Government." One of the soldiers, moved by what he sees, dismounts his horse, kneels on the ground, and kisses it. He then recites a prayer: "O Juchipila, cradle of the revolution of 1910, O blessed land, land steeped in the blood of martyrs, blood of dreamers, the only true men."[7]

Juchipila's historical significance is not only political and military. Even during the precolonial era, it was a center of economic activity for the area's indigenous population. And from the time of the Spanish conquest, Juchipila served as the larger region's market town. It had the good fortune to be located on the fastest road between the large city of Guadalajara to the south and the silver mining area of Zacatecas to the north. In the nineteenth century and previous times, cotton, beans, and corn were the main subsistence crops. In terms of cash crops, sugarcane was the principal one—beginning in the colonial era and through the 1940s. And its associated by-products—raw sugar (*piloncillo*) and cane alcohol (*aguardiente*)—were the chief sources of commercial activity. Trade in these commodities with surrounding areas allowed for the importation of manufactured goods for local consumption.[8]

The soil of the area is generally poor in quality; combined with the region's scarcity of available water, the poor soil severely limits the potential for commercial agriculture. Today, there is little sugarcane grown in and around Juchipila. Instead, the lands are planted largely with alfalfa, oats, corn, and vegetables for local consumption. In terms of commercial agriculture, guayaba (guava) dominates. Others—those owned (or leased) by those with relatively large amounts of capital—are planted with blue agave, a plant indigenous to Mexico that produces a fruit from which tequila is made.

But relatively few Juchipilans today make a living from agriculture. As of 1990, 26.3 percent of the municipio's economically active population worked in agriculture for their livelihoods. Just a decade earlier, the figure was a little more than 50 percent (In 1960, the figure stood at 82 percent.) Like Mexico as a whole, an increasing percentage of the economically active population—about half in the case of Juchipila—works in the commercial and service sectors.[9]

To the casual visitor from the outside, the town of Juchipla looks

Mexican Revolution, Juchipila. Circa 1912. PHOTO COURTESY OF STUDIO GONZALES, JUCHIPILA, ZACATECAS, MEXICO.

prosperous. There are many small- and medium-size businesses as well as numerous big, modern houses—both signs of the dynamic circulation of money. But the impression is somewhat deceptive. Outside of agriculture, almost all of the immediate area's economic activity is for local consumption.[10] Many of the more well-to-do-looking houses are typically unoccupied except during the brief periods when the migrants living in the United States who own them come home to visit. This is especially true in many of the small villages that comprise Juchipila, the municipio, beyond the center of town; there are so few people left in some of them they almost feel deserted—a growing phenomenon in numerous small towns and villages heavily engaged in migration. And much of Juchipila's wealth is generated elsewhere, provided by its sons and daughters who have migrated to the United States and send funds (called remittances) home—often on a regular basis.[11]

In 1990, it was estimated that residents of Juchipila received $5.9 million in remittances.[12] In 1998, the figure reached $7.4 million, outstripping the gross value of agricultural production by 20 percent.[13] Its dependence on remittances—like that on migration—seems to have only grown since that time. One bank manager interviewed in 2004 estimated that 80 to 90 percent of the town's income comes from remittances. "Without migration," he said, "Juchipila would die."[14] A manager of another bank thought the figure was only about 40 percent. But whether the figure is 40 percent or 90 percent, or somewhere in between, there's no question that remittances—and migration—fuel a highly significant slice of Juchipila's economy and help sustain the very existence of the town and its inhabitants. While perhaps somewhat exaggerating the poverty of economic activity in the municipio, Rafael Jimenez Nuñez, Juchipila's mayor, made a similar assessment in 2004:

The economy here in Juchipila has survived for many years, and will continue to survive thanks to the migration of our people to the United States. Practically nothing is produced here. Practically there aren't any types of jobs. The only strong economic movement that you see here in Juchipila and in all of southern Zacatecas—the majority of it—is thanks to the money that is sent by our countrymen to the families that are here, who were left here.[15]

—∿∿—

The creation of migratory links such as those that exist between Juchipila and the United States is never a one-way process. Such ties always involve dynamic interrelationships between "sending" and "receiving" areas. In the Mexico-U.S. case, these interrelationships have long been deeply unequal and have been fueled to a significant degree by patterns of economic investment and restructuring that have led to a concentration of the benefits in the hands of a small number of Mexican elites and investors abroad—especially in the United States.[16]

While dating back to the early to mid-1800s, Mexico-U.S. migration did not become significant in size or in geographical extent until the twentieth century. Prior to that, the scope of migration northward was quite small. Between 1850 and 1900, for example, only about 13,000 Mexicans emigrated to the United States. Over the three decades that followed, by contrast, the number was approximately 728,000.[17]

This dramatic change took place for a number of reasons. First, agricultural policies during the reign of Mexican dictator Porfirio Díaz (1876–1911, during which time he was out of office for a total of approximately four years) discouraged small-scale agriculture through widespread land expropriations, dispossession, privatization and the concentration of holdings in the hands of large-scale landowners who were increasingly relying on mechanized methods, which led to fewer opportunities for paid labor. Together, these changes stimulated out-migration from central Mexico, the area of historic concentration of the country's population. By 1910, more than 95 percent of rural households were without land. Second, transportation improvements within Mexico—specifically regular railroad passenger service between Mexico City and El Paso, Texas that began in 1884 and, in 1888, with the Mexican border towns of Piedras Negras and Nuevo Laredo (across from Eagle Pass and Laredo, Texas, respectively)—greatly facilitated movement toward the United States. And, third, U.S. companies—including the very ones that built and owned the railroads in Mexico[18]—recruited Mexican contract laborers (a violation of the Alien Contract Labor Law of 1885 in the United States), often by using underhanded methods that led to migrant laborers effectively working as indentured servants to pay off loans granted by the recruiters for their passage northward. This laid the basis for the mass migration that would take off in the early twentieth century.[19]

At that time, the U.S. Southwest was the destination for most migrants, but many were increasingly heading to destinations outside of the region as well. By the 1920s, for example, Mexican migrants were working in sugar beets in Minnesota, railroad construction in Kansas, meatpacking in Chicago, coal mining in Oklahoma, automobile manufacturing in Detroit, fish canneries in Alaska, and sharecropping in Louisiana.[20] Immigration from Mexico in the first decade of the 1900s was still modest, however.

Beginning in 1910, the Mexican Revolution led to a significant upsurge in migration to the United States. Many rural Mexicans migrated to urban areas in search of greater physical safety and social stability. Similar reasons informed decisions to migrate across the boundary into the United States. The U.S. government admitted tens of thousands of Mexicans as what were in effect economic refugees between 1911 and 1915. This rise accompanied a great increase in labor demand for and recruitment of Mexican workers. Key to the situation was a shortage of low-wage labor in the U.S. Southwest. A variety of factors contributed to the regional labor shortage: the out-migration of poor white and black laborers to the cities of the northern United States; the 1907–08 "Gentlemen's Agreement" between the U.S. and Japan by which Tokyo agreed to not issue passports to Japanese citizens wishing to emigrate to the United States to work and issue them only to wives, parents, and children of Japanese immigrants already in the United States; the U.S. entry into World War I; and the passage of restrictive legislation in the form of the Immigration Act of 1917 (which exempted Mexicans).[21]

The decade of the 1920s saw Mexican migration reach a new high. A long-simmering conflict between the Mexican state and the Catholic Church erupted into an armed insurrection, the so-called Cristero Rebellion, causing thousands of workers to emigrate. The completion of a railroad between Guadalajara, Jalisco, in central Mexico, and Nogales, Arizona, in 1927 further facilitated new migration. Almost 500,000 Mexicans entered the United States on visas during the decade.[22] By some estimates, more than 10 percent of Mexico's entire population was living in the United States by 1930.[23] Much of the migration was circular in nature, with migrants frequently moving back and forth between the two countries.

While during the 1930s the migratory flow temporarily slowed down and reversed as a result of the mass deportations and the drastic economic downturn in the United States—in California's Imperial Valley, for instance, the amount of lettuce and cantaloupe shipped from

Juchipila, Zacatecas, Mexico. January 2002. Julio César Gallegos's sixth grade photo from la Escuela Francisco Madero.

the region declined by 50 percent between 1929 and 1933[24]—the beginning of the Bracero Program (actually a series of programs) in 1942 helped bring it back to life. Over its twenty-two years of existence, the program resulted in U.S. authorities' contracting out approximately 5 million braceros to growers and ranchers in twenty-four states.[25] The Bracero Program was terminated in 1964, however, for a variety of reasons—ranging from opposition from religious groups (such as the National Council of Churches and the National Catholic Welfare Conference) and organized labor critical of what they saw as the highly abusive and exploitative nature of the program, to reduced demand for braceros because of the rapid mechanization of cotton harvesting (no agricultural sector employed more braceros).[26]

But the ending of the Bracero Program did little to reduce migration. As before, migration—independent of formal mechanisms of recruitment—continued. Given the mutual interdependence between U.S. employers, especially in agriculture, and Mexican sending communities, and the deeply embedded nature of these ties, the previously legal migratory stream simply went underground. There had previously been "illegal" migration, of course, but it increased significantly—a process facilitated greatly by economic restructuring in Mexico beginning in the mid-1960s that saw the country's "economic miracle" come to a close, considerable capital flight, the devaluation of the peso in 1976, and the fall of oil prices in 1982. And, beginning in the mid-1980s, Mexican elites initiated a process of deregulation, privatization, and trade expansion that involved a reduction in tariffs for imports, a dismantling of many subsidies, and an opening up of the economy to foreign trade and investment—a process very much encouraged by U.S. officials and one that culminated in the implementation of the North American Free Trade Agreement (NAFTA) in 1994.[27]

Together, these developments strengthened and expanded the ties between Mexico and the United States: between 1993 and 2004, U.S.-Mexico trade more than tripled in value, from $89.5 billion to $275.3 billion. While Mexico depends far more on the United States for its economic health than vice versa, the two economies are tightly intertwined—so much so that a 2006 publication of the Federal Reserve Bank of Dallas characterized them as "increasingly synchronized," while asserting that they "now march almost in lockstep."[28] Yet, at the same time, these developments have undermined the livelihoods of many in Mexico—a NAFTA-related trade deficit, one in favor of the United States,[29] for example, contributed significantly to the loss of an estimated 1.3 million jobs in Mexico's agricultural sector between 1994 and 2002—thus encouraging large numbers of Mexicans to migrate across the boundary.[30] Today, about 10 percent of Mexico's population (people born in Mexico who are still alive) resides in the United States. About 15 percent of Mexico's labor force is employed in its neighbor to the north—in a wide variety of occupations, with over half working in construction and the service sector, and only about 4 percent working in farming, fishing, or forestry. Approximately one out of every seven Mexican workers migrates to the United States.[31]

These workers are a huge source of income for Mexico as a whole: in 2006, Mexicans living in the United States sent $24 billion to their loved ones in Mexico, making remittances second to oil as a source of foreign income for the country.[32]

—⁓⁓—

Juchipila was caught up in the Mexico–United States migratory stream from very early on. It is unclear when migration from Juchipila began exactly, but it probably commenced in the context of the Revolution as many fled the area's intense bloodshed and destruction for the United States.[33] Certainly by the time Julio's father, Don Florentino Gallegos, traveled to the U.S. Southwest for the first time in 1937, strong migratory links were already in place between the United States and the Mexican state of Zacatecas.

The roots of the migratory ties lie in Zacatecas's development as an important center of economic activity for the Spanish Empire. After defeating the Caxcanes, an indigenous group, in the area of Juchipila in 1542, the Spanish established the city of Zacatecas to the north in 1546 as part of their quest for silver. This led to ancillary economic activities nearby—such as lumbering, cattle raising, and farming—to support the mines. By the mid-1700s, Zacatecas was supplying one-fifth of the world's silver, but its forests and pastures were close to ruin owing to depletion. At the same time, discoveries of silver deposits elsewhere threatened the region's dominance. Such factors, combined with the destruction and disruptions associated with the war for independence from Spain, which began in 1811, led to a gradual decline of the state's economy. While large-scale farming in the form of haciendas subsequently emerged, such development was not sufficient to keep Zacatecans at home as many migrated toward the north of the country in the last decades of the 1800s.[34]

A steady flow of migrants from Zacatecas, and from other states in Mexico's densely populated central plateau (states such as Jalisco and Michoacán) to the United States began in the 1880s. But, according to Raúl Delgado Wise and Miguel Moctezuma Longoria—both scholars at the Autonomous University of Zacatecas—the year 1900 was key in terms of fueling out-migration. It was then that prices for the state's minerals went into a free fall. Silver was particularly impacted, its value declining to less that half that of 1873. This had the effect of marginalizing small-scale miners and facilitating the rise of more "modern," large-scale enterprises dependent on new (labor-reducing) technologies in the mining sector. As a result, overall employment in the sector declined dramatically. The number of mine workers in Zacatecas in 1893, for instance, was 16,459; by 1910, there were only 9,769. This, combined with a significant and associated increase in poverty in the state, led to out-migration—largely to other parts of Mexico, but also to the United States to a notable degree.[35] Also contributing, in addition to the damage done to small-scale agriculture by the Porfiriato (the period of Porfirio Díaz's reign), was a drought in 1907–10 that wiped out much of the corn harvest in states such as Zacatecas, creating famine-like conditions in many areas.[36]

The years of the Mexican Revolution led to an even greater out-migration, with the state's population declining by an annual average of 2.3 percent between 1910 and 1921, a development very much tied to a severe deterioration of the Zacatecas economy. The disruption of semifeudal agricultural relations and the reduction in investment in mining brought about by the war coincided with a series of strikes in the mines, which were virtually paralyzed. In the words of geographer Richard Jones, "If [Mexican] independence brought production to a temporary halt, revolution destroyed productive capital and land so that production was decimated for years to come."[37] Warring troops seized grain and, stole, sold, or consumed most of the state's livestock, burned fields, and pillaged and destroyed sugar and mescal mills, their actions leading to the abandonment of mining and many large farms, and turning Zacatecas into an economic wasteland.[38]

Juchipila was, most likely, profoundly affected by the destruction. As Mariano Azuela described in *The Underdogs*, the town itself, like so many in the area, was "in ruins." Painting a picture that belies any romantic notions of the Revolution, Azuela wrote how the "black trail of incendiaries showed in the roofless houses, in the burnt arcades. Almost all the houses were closed, yet here and there, those still open offered, in ironic contrast, portals gaunt and bare as the white skeletons of horses scattered over the roads. The terrible pangs of hunger seemed to speak from every face."[39]

Mexico had little time to recover from the devastation associated with the Revolution, an extremely bloody episode that led to one million deaths and the devastation of much of the country's agriculture. In its aftermath, armed bands associated with various factions—or who claimed to be—continued to attack and plunder in the countryside. And in 1926 the Cristero Rebellion broke out when peasants in Zacatecas and nearby states rose up to resist what they perceived as the revolutionary government's hostility toward the Catholic Church.[40] The three-year conflict, which the government eventually won, resulted in tens of thousands of deaths. As during the Revolution, the north central states, which include Zacatecas, bore the lion's share of the violence, further impoverishing Zacatecas's economy and overall social fabric.[41]

The gains of the Revolution did lead to agrarian reform and significant land redistribution within Zacatecas and Mexico more broadly, allowing for a far greater number of individuals and families to participate in farming—both collectively and individually. Between the time of the Revolution and 1940, land redistribution resulted in the creation throughout Mexico of more than 13,000 *ejidos*, comprising more than thirty-one million hectares of land distributed to approximately 1.7 million peasants.[42] Nonethleless, in Zacatecas and other places the agricultural reforms did not bring about the type of changes that would allow most farmers to move beyond the subsistence level. Instead, the carving up of large landholdings led to small, inadequate plots. Moreover, most farmers lived in isolated, rural communities, and were still subject to the vagaries of nature (in the form of occasional drought, for example). And government assistance programs in terms of credit, agricultural extension, and seeds were at best inadequate, and more often nonexistent.[43]

In this context, migration from Zacatecas to the United States increased sharply in the 1940s. The establishment of the Bracero Program played a huge role in this process as U.S. agricultural interests—in conjunction with elements of the Mexican state—recruited and contracted workers, thus facilitating ever-stronger migratory links. Leobardo Reynoso, as governor of Zacatecas in the latter half of the 1940s and the state's dominant political actor for the next few decades, greatly facilitated the flow of braceros from places like Juchipila, where he was born and raised, to the United States. He played a key role in mediating between U.S. contractors who visited Zacatecas in search of laborers, and individuals interested in working as braceros.[44]

Such recruitment and the Mexican state's cooperation in bringing it about helped to intensify the migratory links between Juchipila and the United States. As elsewhere, the migratory stream took on a life of its own to a significant extent, a development facilitated by economic transformations involving a decline in employment opportunities in agriculture. During the period of 1986–91, for example, about 55 percent of men in Juchipila born between 1952 and 1973 spent at least one month living and working in the United States. Among women, the corresponding figure was much lower, hovering a little below 10 percent, but still significant.[45]

⁓⁓⁓

Today, one can find Zacatecans—and Juchipilans—throughout the United States. In terms of migrants from Zacatecas as a whole, California and Illinois are the most popular points of settlement. For Juchipilans, there are no authoritative studies of where they go to work and live in the United States, but there is little question that the biggest share by far is concentrated in and around Los Angeles. And it was in and around Los Angeles that Don Florentino and his children eventually settled.

Julio's father, Don Florentino Gallegos first went to the United States in 1937 when he was only about 14 years old. Arriving in the San Diego area where he worked for a number of years picking peaches, tomatoes, avocados, and lettuce, it would be about five years before he returned to Juchipila. It was then, at 19 years of age, that he got married for the first time.

When he returned to the United States, he got a job working with the railroad, work that took him to Nevada, Arizona, and California. But, like so many Mexican migrants, he would travel back and forth between Mexico and the United States, spending extended periods of time in both places. During his time in Juchipila, he got married

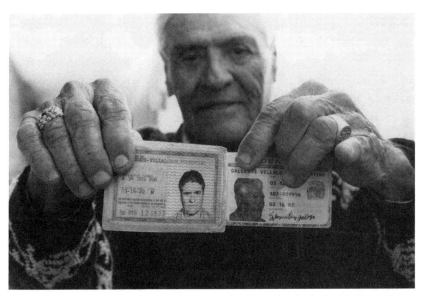

Juchipila, Zacatecas, Mexico. January 2002. Don Florentino displaying his first and most recent U.S. "Resident Alien" cards.

twice (both his wives died while he was still married to them) and was later *juntado*—a common-law relationship—with another woman, Consuelo Durán, the mother of Julio and his brother, Juan Florentino (known as "Tino"). He also served as a policeman in the town for a period of time.

Most of Don Florentino's time in the United States was spent in and around Los Angeles—where he also worked for the railroad for a time. His settlement there and his movement back and forth between L.A. and Juchipila were hardly novel given the long-standing ties between the storied City of Angels and greater Mexico.

These dynamic linkages originated with the arrival of Franciscan missionaries in Los Angeles in 1769. (A Portuguese explorer had previously arrived there and claimed the area for the Spanish Empire in 1542.) They established a mission nearby in what is today known as the San Gabriel Valley. Prior to and through that era, indigenous peoples—Tongva (later called Gabrieleños), Chumash, and others—had inhabited the region. A little more than a decade later, in 1781, eleven families, a group of approximately forty to fifty individuals—of African, Native American, Spanish, and mixed descent—associated with the mission, established a colonial Spanish outpost in the form of an agricultural settlement near what is today called the Los Angeles River to help strengthen Spanish control of what was then Alta California. It was named *El pueblo de nuestra Señora la Reina de los Angeles*, the village of Our Lady the Queen of the Angels, and would later be called simply Los Angeles. At the time, an estimated 5,000 native people lived in the Los Angeles basin.[46]

For decades, Los Angeles was a small ranch town. In 1800, its population was only 315. In the late 1820s, a French visitor noted that it had only eighty-two houses. By the 1830s—by which time the city had developed into Alta California's political, economic, and social center—it had a population of just under 1,000 inhabitants. In the immediate aftermath of the American takeover of California in 1848, the population of Los Angeles was still relatively small. In 1850, people of Mexican descent numbered 1,215 while the Anglo population was less than 300. Until 1860, Mexicans remained in the majority. But soon Los Angeles would become a full-fledged "American" city.[47]

As throughout southern California, the arrival of the railroad in the 1870s and additional lines in the 1880s facilitated the demise of Mexican dominance in Los Angeles. Between 1850 and 1880, the city's Mexican population increased to 2,166 whereas the Anglo population grew to about 8,000 during the same period. Within another ten years, the city's population had exploded to 50,395, the Mexican-origin population only having grown slightly.[48] By 1900, the population was over 100,000 within the city itself—only 817 of whom had been born in Mexico according to the U.S. Census—with another 70,000 inhabitants in the surrounding county.[49]

An inextricable part of the process of Americanization of Los Angeles involved the marginalization of the Mexican-origin population and the erasure of its Mexican past—a process of whitewashing, in the words of historian William Deverell. It was a process that was frequently quite violent, a continuation of the conquest that made Los Angeles "American," at least nominally, in the first place. As Deverell writes of Los Angeles in the 1850s, "What had been the Mexican American War only a few years earlier became a war against Mexican Americans."[50]

As in Texas, some of the Mexican elite in California had supported joining the United States. But their enthusiasm for the new order quickly faded as its racist reality became increasingly evident. American settlers—who typically saw themselves as improvers of the land, as developers of an efficient, profitable agricultural economy that the Spanish mission system and its Mexican offspring had failed to bring about—took over much of the land of the *Californios* (Spanish-speaking inhabitants of Alta California), often employing harassment and intim-idation, and sometimes outright violence. In response to Anglo squatters, the California legislature passed a bill in 1851 which allowed them to occupy land that "to the best of one's knowledge" was unused, while creating a commission to investigate the validity of Mexican land grants in the state. The legislation put the burden of proof on the landowners. This—combined with high taxes, a drop in cattle prices, disastrous weather in the early 1860s, and violence and intimidation by Anglo settlers—led to a rapid decline in Mexican land ownership throughout California. This was especially within the city limits of Los Angeles where land was more valuable. While more than 61 percent of the city's Mexican families owned land or some type of property in 1850, the figure declined to less than 22 percent by 1870.[51]

In terms of the non-elite Mexican population, a whole host of measures in the wake of the Gold Rush discriminated against them in the mines. More broadly, Mexicans were often cheated out of their wages through a two-tier system that systematically underpaid them in comparison to Anglo workers. And in the name of law and order, violence—sometimes murderous—toward Mexicans on the part of local officials and vigilante groups was common in the southern part of the state, especially in and around Los Angeles.[52]

While the 1880s were a time of economic prosperity for Los Ange-les, Mexicans were effectively excluded from the city's transformation from a small town to a modern metropolis. The emerging economic order froze Mexicans into a position of subordination, making upward mobility extremely difficult. As before, most Mexicans worked as manual laborers while a relatively small percentage of Ang-los did so. At the same time, the segregation of Mexicans increased, as did their political marginalization. By 1873, for example, the par-ticipation of Mexicans on juries, and in formal political processes more generally, became increasingly rare.[53]

As large numbers of Anglos from elsewhere in the United States migrated to Los Angeles in the late 1800s, the city's ruling classes residentially segregated Mexicans while providing them with sub-par services and infrastructure. An 1874 municipal ordinance, for example, restricted brothels to the Mexican section of the city.[54] At that time, much of the Mexican population lived in the area around La Placita, a public park that is also the birthplace of Los Angeles, sharing a neighborhood—derisively referred to as Sonora Town by Anglos—with mostly Chinese.

Such institutionalized inequality laid the basis for the apartheid-like structures that would shape the Mexican experience in Los Angeles in the early twentieth century when immigration from Mexico into the city and its surrounding areas took off in the context of Mexico's civil war. Los Angeles became a refuge not only for those fleeing forced conscription, economic chaos, and violence associated with the conflict, but also for elements who played an important role in the struggle against Mexico's established order.

The resulting growth was dramatic: in the period 1910–20, the city of Los Angeles's Mexican population grew from 5,000 to 30,000. By 1930, it increased to more than 97,000, with another 70,000 in the county.[55]

During this time ideas of Anglo superiority were front and center and very much in the air of Los Angeles. As one of the victors of the city's 1924 poetry contest wrote in his award-winning poem, "Dominion over land and sea of this enduring Race—Supreme Historic Prophecy—is now in final consummation."[56] Hence, while elites in Los Angeles welcomed Mexican migrants as laborers, they simultaneously constructed them as permanent outsiders. Mexicans were only desirable to the extent they offered needed resources. As Robert McLean, a local religious leader, stated in 1929, "In Los Angeles and, indeed, in many communities, it is the Mexican[s] who do the common labor. In fact, we have imported them for that very purpose."[57] And they fulfilled that purpose admirably. According to Dr. George Clements, a "Mexican expert" and the manager of the Los Angeles Chamber of Commerce's Agricultural Department, "No labor that has ever come to the United States is more satisfactory under righteous treatment. The Mexican as the result of years of servitude, has always looked upon his employer as his patron and upon himself as part of the establishment."[58]

Despite such praise, it was also widely perceived that Mexicans were a potential source of danger, for which the dominant classes of Los Angeles and California as a whole had to have various tools of redress in case any such dangers were to arise. The nature of the threats, as well as the instruments of control, ranged from the epidemiological to the outright repressive. As the very same Dr. Clements reminded California's governor in 1927, "the Mexican laborer is an alien possible of deportation should he become indigent or a social menace."[59] All the while, many southern Californian elites endeavored to convince themselves and others that Mexican migrants were not there to stay, but would naturally return to Mexico due to their homing-pigeon-like instinct.[60] Yet, by 1930 Los Angeles was by far the largest "Mexican city" in the United States.[61] And it was becoming increasingly clear that many people of Mexican origin in L.A. were not footloose migrants, but people who intended to remain.

This fact, combined with Mexicans' outsider status, helped to make Los Angeles a focal point for the mass deportations during Great Depression of the 1930s. There, the raids, write Francisco Balderrama and Raymond Rodríguez, "assumed the logistics of full-scale paramilitary operations. Federal officers, county deputy sheriffs, and city police cooperated in local roundups in order to assure maximum success. Scare tactics, rumors and propaganda were adroitly used in creating a climate of fear." A key part of the effort was the February 26, 1931, raid on La Placita, a symbolic and social center of the city's Mexican community. Immigration agents blocked all of the park's entrances and demanded that everyone produce a passport and some evidence of authorized entry and residency in the United States.[62] Such efforts—which dovetailed with campaigns by local officials and businessmen to rid California of its Mexican population—contributed significantly to one-third of Mexicans in Los Angeles leaving and returning to Mexico during the decade.[63]

One of those campaigns led to the characterizations of Mexicans as prone to tuberculosis, because of supposed biological propensity, and as especially reliant on welfare programs. In response, the Los Angeles County Department of Charities established a "Transportation Section" (also known as the Deportation Section) charged with finding unauthorized Mexican migrants who were receiving county-sponsored medical aid. From 1931 to 1933, the department deported more than 13,000 Mexicans to Mexico. It is likely that many deportees were authorized migrants or citizens.[64]

While members of Los Angeles's business class supported the deportations, they were also confident that they could lure the Mexicans back to the area were the need to arise—which it soon did. But the social boundary between people of Mexican origin and European Americans did not simply come and go. The "war propaganda" employed during the 1930s deportations (which included the expulsion of tens of thousands of U.S. citizens of Mexican descent), in fact, merely "reinforced in the minds of many Euroamericans the idea of Mexicans as 'aliens' and 'the other,'" writes historian Rodolfo Acuña—no less so in Los Angeles.[65]

People of Mexican ancestry in California remained second-class citizens throughout the World War II years. Mexicans generally occupied the worst housing stock, with blatant discrimination contributing to a form of residential apartheid in places such as Los Angeles.[66] Segregation was common, with many recreational facilities formally excluding Mexican Americans.[67] And in the aftermath of the mass internment of Japanese Americans during World War II, Mexicans became the target once again of nativist sentiment in California. Institutionalized subordination facilitated the criminalization of Mexicans, especially youths. Both law enforcement and numerous academic specialists had long defined the Mexican-origin population as especially prone to delinquent behavior; such perceptions contributed to a number of ugly incidents of violence directed against the community. The most infamous case was the so-called Zoot-Suit Riots in June 1943 when thousands of U.S. military personnel, along with many civilians, attacked Mexican Americans—mostly youths— in East Los Angeles over the period of several days, supposedly as

Lennox, California, U.S.A. September 2001. Memorial to Julio shown to us at Tino's house.

part of a battle against "hoodlums."[68] Local police aided and abetted the rioters, doing little to nothing to stop the violence. Indeed, they arrested more than 600 Mexican-American youths, but only a small number of military members. All the while the *Los Angeles Times* and other local media fanned the flames of vigilante violence.[69]

Yet these events also occurred at a time when racist sentiment was changing.[70] Biologically based theories of racial inferiority were falling out of favor. Local Los Angeles officials, for instance, were very defensive in responding to charges of racism from critics of the riots.[71] Still, dominant groups persisted in marginalizing Mexican Americans and recent Mexican immigrants. During the 1950s, for example, Los Angeles city officials evicted the residents and destroyed all the homes in a "blighted," almost exclusively Mexican community near downtown called Chávez Ravine. (Often done in the name of "urban renewal," such "urban cleansing" was a common tactic employed by local elites across the United States as a way of ridding city cores of unwanted residents and neighborhoods.) Built in its place was the stadium for a baseball team moving from Brooklyn, New York, the one today known as the Los Angeles Dodgers.[72] During this time, specifically in 1954, the Los Angeles Police Department, the Los Angeles County Sheriff's Office, and other local police agencies worked with the Immigration Service in its arrests and deportations of unauthorized "aliens" as part of Operation Wetback.[73] In addition, powerful institutions in the area continued to criminalize Mexican-American youths, with the police and the larger justice system constructing young people of Mexican descent as inherently violent and crime-prone, and treating them accordingly.[74]

The Civil Rights and Chicano movements of the 1960s, and the growing demographic and political power of Mexican Americans, helped to bring about a significant decline in the expression of overtly racist sentiment by local elites. At the same time, harsh, large-scale state measures against people of Mexican descent became far less common. And people of Mexican origin were increasingly able to access power as evidenced by the presence of Latinos on the Los Angeles City Council (but not until 1985), among other elite institutions.

Nevertheless, Los Angeles remained, and remains, a deeply divided city, part of a deeply divided state. Given its huge foreign-born, noncitizen population, large sections of the city are disenfranchised. In several of Los Angeles's congressional districts, for example, over half the population are noncitizens and thus ineligible to vote.[75] Yet, citizenship as a de jure category also carries insufficient weight. Los Angeles' Mexican-origin population is heavily concentrated in the eastern and, to a lesser extent, southern portions of the city, just as is a disproportionate amount of the city's poverty, unemployment, and violence. Traversing the divide between these urban areas, writes journalist Marc Cooper, is "almost as jarring as going from San Diego across the international border. On our Westside, almost exclusively, are those who are served. To their east and south, those who do the serving."[76]

Such residential segregation is a principal structural feature of the United States, argue sociologists Douglas Massey and Nancy Denton, and has long been so. As in the case of apartheid South Africa, they contend, it is tied to a larger system of race-based injustice in that it both reflects and helps to create the deep racial socioeconomic divides that plague American society.[77] In this sense, Los Angeles, one of the most segregated of U.S. cities,[78] is hardly unique. But it is distinct given its relationship to all things Mexican, its huge Mexican-origin population (much of which is unauthorized)—many call Los Angeles the second-biggest "Mexican" city in world after Mexico City—its high immigrant population, and its intense, historically deep and profoundly unequal ties to Mexico and beyond.

It was into this Los Angeles that Julio César Gallegos arrived in 1993. But he did not arrive in the City of Angels proper, but in a small adjacent city on its southern boundary: Inglewood. Inglewood is a city that mirrors L.A.'s apartheid history, but in a way that differs from the Mexican-Anglo dichotomy: today Inglewood is known by many as an African American city—despite its very substantial Latino population. Yet it is one where blacks were effectively not able to reside until the second half of the 1960s.

In the 1920s, an investigation following a shoot-out between members of the Ku Klux Klan and an Inglewood police officer revealed that three of the Klansmen were city police officers.[79] Such overt racism was hardly exclusive to Inglewood around and within the metropolis of Los Angeles. While the very founding of Los Angeles is owed significantly to people of African heritage—the majority of the original settlers in 1792 were at least in part of African descent[80]— and conditions in L.A. for blacks were much better than in the South and in many industrial cities of the North, Los Angeles was, says historian Douglas Flamming, "an oddly half-free environment."[81] L.A. African Americans had to endure everyday forms of racism—overt, institutionalized, or de facto—for most of the twentieth century. It was not until 1956, for example, that the city's fire stations were integrated, and even after that many black firefighters had to endure deep discrimination and abuse within their workplaces.[82]

Of the various manifestations of antiblack racism, residential segregation was perhaps the most visible and telling.[83] Inglewood embodied such segregation more than most. While as early as the first decade of the 1900s, it had a sizable community of Japanese descent (many of them were small farmers),[84] the 1950 census showed a population that was only .3 percent "non-white." The city was not at all welcoming to would-be black residents and was the last "hold-out" among the white working-class and middle-class cities on the southern edge of Los Angeles. The 1960 census, for example, counted only twenty-nine "Negroes" in Inglewood's population of 63,390, and there were no black children in the city's public schools. It was an extremely difficult place for African Americans—and, to a significant, but lesser degree, Latinos[85]—to buy homes as real estate agents "steered" them away, and residents used a wide variety of techniques to maintain racial purity in their neighborhoods. It was also rumored that blacks should not be on the city's streets at night, which effectively served as a curfew.[86] It was not until the 1966 rebellion in neighboring South Los Angeles—often known as the Watts Riot or Uprising—that whites began moving out of Inglewood, opening up residential space. As largely middle-class blacks moved into the city— about 10,000 by 1970—many among the white parents who remained were highly resistant to integrating the public schools. It took a federal court order to change that, leading to crosstown busing and high levels of tension and violence in some of the schools.[87] By 1980, more than half the city's population was black as most whites fled to other areas.[88] By 1990, the city's white population was less than 9 percent.

The racial-demographic shift often led to characterizations and depictions of Inglewood—in the Los Angeles area and nationally— that were, at best, simplistic and unflattering. In the 1992 high-profile, Hollywood feature film *Grand Canyon*, for instance, Inglewood is one of the few specific places actually mentioned. The film portrays Los Angeles as metropolitan area characterized by wide racial and class gaps and random violence. But it is Inglewood where the movie opens and where most of its most disturbing moments take place. In addition to showing it as the site of the Great Western Forum, the then-home of the Los Angeles Lakers, Inglewood is depicted as an exclusively African American city menaced by thugs and gangbangers.

In the film, Danny Glover plays a tow-truck driver who rescues Kevin Kline. Stuck in traffic after attending a Lakers game, Kline decides to take detour only to have his car break down on a desolate Inglewood street where he is accosted and threatened by five menacing-looking black men, one of whom displays a pistol.

"This neighborhood had gone to shit," Glover tells Kline after extricating him from the potentially dangerous situation. "You're lucky you got out with your life," Kline's 15-year-old son opines when he learned that his father's car had broken down there, suggesting that Inglewood's reputation for deadly violence is a fact of life.

Julio arrived in Inglewood one year later, one year after the Los Angeles riots, in a city that looked very different from the one depicted in *Grand Canyon*. While Inglewood is an African American city in many ways, it is also a Latino—and specifically Mexican—one as well. Today blacks and Latinos have roughly equal shares of the city's population (about 47 percent each) of approximately 110,000, with few Anglos remaining. It certainly has gang problems and, in some areas, high levels of poverty and unemployment, but is also largely a solidly middle-class city, with single-family homes on well-kept streets.[89] Julio's half brother, Jesús, who owns a successful lawn-care business, and his wife, Vicky—also a Juchipila native—live on one of those streets in a house where Don Florentino used to stay on his many visits to Los Angeles after retiring and returning to Juchipila. Julio also lived in the house when he first migrated to Los Angeles. In addition, Inglewood also has a Juchipila hometown association, which, like other such organizations, helps to fund infrastructure and social programs in Mexico, as well as economic development projects, as a way of lessening the need to emigrate.[90]

Julio did not stay in Inglewood for long. Through a half brother named Pedro, he soon ended up working for M. L. M. Amusements, a company that staged carnivals throughout southern California, running a coin-toss booth. It was there in 1994 that he met Jackie who was also working for the company, selling corndogs and popcorn. They started going out—it was love at first sight, according to Jackie—and soon got engaged. In October 1995, they got married.

By that time, Julio was already living nearby in Jackie's neighborhood, Boyle Heights, a historic neighborhood next to downtown L.A., just east of the Los Angeles River. It is the city of Los Angeles's portion of what is called "East Los Angeles"—what a 1981 article in the *New Yorker* magazine characterized as a "Spanish-speaking city, a Mexican-American and Mexican city, stretching twenty miles or more east of the river and perhaps fifteen miles along it."[91]

Originally known as Paredón Blanco (White Bluff), Boyle Heights came about in the 1870s as Los Angeles grew to include the east side of the river that shares the city's moniker. It was renamed after Andrew Boyle, a wealthy Irish immigrant and the first Anglo to reside on the eastside. The area became attractive to the city's burgeoning professional class with the arrival of the railroads in the 1870s and 1880s, by which time about 300 to 400 businessmen and their families lived there, then an exclusive, rural community with few Mexicans.[92] As immigrants continued to arrive in the city and Boyle Heights became increasingly linked to it via transportation and infrastructural ties, the neighborhood effectively became a residential port of entry into Los Angeles as working-class Jews, Armenians, and Japanese settled there. By the mid-1920s, a number of middle- and upper-class Mexicans lived in the neighborhood. During the next decade, working- and middle-class Mexicans began moving into the area in large numbers, further diversifying the neighborhood. And in the 1940s, the city constructed public housing there, which led to

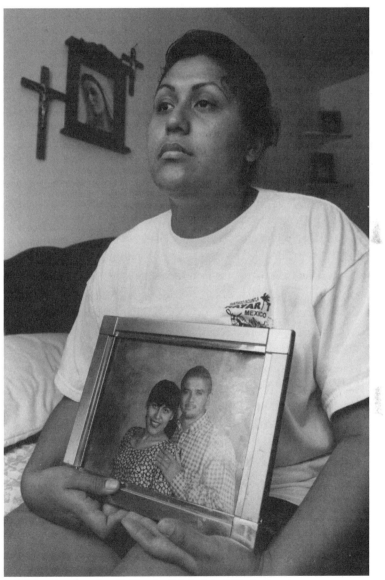

Boyle Heights, Los Angeles, California, U.S.A. July 2001. Jackie at home.

blacks moving into Boyle Heights. That time period marked the apex of the area's multiethnic nature, however. By the mid-1940s, many Jews began moving out of the Heights—what had hitherto been the center of Jewish life in Los Angeles—for the city's exclusively white Westside, while the area's once large Japanese population had declined significantly owing to the federal government's removal and internment of people of Japanese-descent during World War II.[93]

Still, two articles in national publications in the mid-1950s characterized Boyle Heights as a locale of ethnic and racial diversity and pluralistic democracy in action. One stated, "few districts in America are as ethnically dynamic, religiously and politically tolerant, and community proud," while another, entitled "U.N. in Microcosm," highlighted Boyle Heights as an exemplar of interethnic cooperation, specifically mentioning the productive ties between the well-established, but quickly dwindling Jewish community and the soon-to-be majority of Mexican-origin residents.[94] Such ties combined with a strong tradition of working-class and radical politics in the Eastside neighborhood's Jewish community explain why, while much of southern California was becoming more politically conservative during that time period, Boyle Heights was a dynamic center of liberal and left-progressive political activism. It was one that embraced and left a legacy of "political interracialism, commitment to civil rights, and a radical multiculturalism," in the words of historian and neighborhood native son George Sánchez.[95]

Despite such levels of democratic coexistence, Boyle Heights's population of Mexican ancestry did not avoid the insecurities associated with being part of a population with a very conditional and precarious relationship with the larger national society. As late as the 1960s, it was a place where Mexico-origin families had to worry about their children being detained and deported to Mexico by U.S. authorities, even if the children were U.S. citizens by birth.[96]

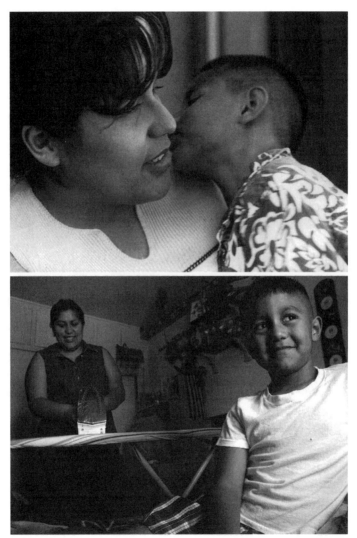

Boyle Heights, Los Angeles, California, U.S.A. (Top) Jackie and Julio Jr., 2001, and (bottom) Jackie and Andrew, 2004.

"Sometimes Junior will ask me for his daddy, and I'll tell him that 'El está con Jesucito en el cielo.' And he'll say, 'Oh yeah, en el sky.'" —Jackie.

Nor did Boyle Heights escape the forced segregation of the larger region of which it was part, and the related patterns of discrimination. The neighborhood's Wyvernwood Apartments—which had been built in 1939 for middle-income people—generally refused to rent to anyone other than whites through the late 1940s, for example.[97] It was into one of these apartments that Jackie, her parents—both Mexican immigrants—and siblings moved in 1976. And as the neighborhood's composition changed, as it became more Latino, the availability of public services declined.[98] Indeed, Boyle Height's very existence as "a polyglot community for most of the twentieth century"[99] was significantly due to the fact that there were many areas of greater Los Angeles where its residents—especially its black and Mexican ones—were not allowed to live.[100] It was not until the mid-1960s, for example, that someone of Mexican descent was able to overcome the restrictive housing covenants and buy a home in South Pasadena.[101]

The history of Roosevelt High School, the public educational destination of most Boyle Heights adolescents—and from where Jackie graduated in 1992—reflects the neighborhood's complicated demographic history. Opened in 1923, its student body was then about 90 percent Jewish, with "a mixture of other ethnic groups, including Mexican-Americans, Armenians, and Russians."[102] The school quickly established itself as a place of tolerance and cooperation across ethno-racial boundaries. In the early 1930s, for instance, Roosevelt elected a student body president of Japanese descent and an African American female class president—without any objections being raised. According to a 1936 survey, the student body was what it classified as 28 percent American, 26 percent Jewish, 24 percent Mexican, 7 percent Russian, 6 percent Japanese, and 9 percent Italian, Armenian, or of some other ethnicity.[103] By the eve of World War II, it was a place where no ethno-racial group had a majority, or dominated the school's leadership positions. Students celebrated this diversity, calling the school "a crucible of all nations. Russians, Jews, Japanese, Mexican, Chinese, Negro," while stating that "all help to make their school the better for having been there."[104] But the school's diversity suffered a big blow in 1942 when the 400 Japanese American students were forcibly removed and sent to internment camps by the federal government.[105] This and larger demographic shifts led to a growing Mexicanization of Roosevelt. By 1968, at the time of Chicano movement, Boyle Heights's population was sufficiently of Mexican descent that groups like the Brown Berets and United Mexican American Students helped to organize "blowouts"— demonstrations in the form of student walkouts—at the school to protest teacher racism, poor facilities, and a curriculum that paid insufficient heed to issues of concern to the Mexican-origin population.[106] By 1980, Roosevelt's population was over 90 percent of Mexican ancestry, with a small number of black and Asian-origin students, and a few of the descendants of Boyle Heights's original Russian settlers. At that time, about 450 students who had just migrated from Mexico entered the school each year, and about 62 percent of the graduates went on to higher education. Yet the dropout rate over the course of four years was about 50 percent, reflecting the transient nature of the student population and the difficult socioeconomic circumstances of their families. Today, the school is about 98 percent Latino.[107]

At the time of the Chicano movement, East Los Angeles was by far the most Mexican of L.A.'s areas with 95 percent of the residents of Mexican descent. It was also an area with a significantly lower average income than the rest of the city. The poverty in Boyle Heights was even more pronounced, with median family income only 54 percent that of Los Angeles County as a whole.[108] However East Los Angeles, in the words of legal scholar Ian Haney López, "was not blighted and hopeless," but rather "relatively settled and stable" with high levels of owner-occupied homes and far fewer immigrants among its population than one might have expected: about 85 percent of the Mexican-origin population were U.S. citizens by birth. It was at the time "a working-class community afflicted by the usual hardships of poverty, poor infrastructure, and scarce jobs."[109]

Today it continues to be.

Julio was very much part of that working-class community—from 1994 when he first moved there until 1998 when he died. He worked there—in the nearby, small industrial city of Vernon[110]—in Colonel Lee's where he prepared Chinese frozen food for minimum wage

Montebello, California, U.S.A. June 2005. Father's Day visit to Resurrection Cemetery.

"Beloved Son, Husband, Father, and Brother. I never thought that this moment would arrive. We never said goodbye. It is difficult to accept this, but God decided matters in this way. I would prefer to know of you far away, but still around in this life. Now it is too late to tell you how much we miss you, but knowing that some day we will see each other again motivates me to continue forward with our sons. Your heart will always live in me because Julio Jr. and Andrew form our love. Julio, we will remember you always and may the Virgin of Guadalupe guide you to find the road to glory."

($5.15 per hour).[111] In addition, he was a neighbor, husband, and father there—to Julio Jr. who was born in early 1996.

But he was also "illegal" and Mexican, and living in what is, in terms of power relations, an American city, one whose contemporary creation is inextricably linked to the U.S. annexation of California and the conquest of the Southwest, and whose political separation from Juchipila, Zacatecas was produced by the imposition of the modern-day boundary. And it was these characteristics that ultimately trumped the others. They effectively made him a criminal—at least according to the dictates of U.S. authorities—forcing Julio to go outside of the legal channels, to traverse dangerous physical terrain to reunite with his family in a place where he did not have official authorization to be. And, given his second-class status, they helped to bring about his low wages which did not allow him to earn enough to pay the fees and fines needed to regularize his presence in the country. Together, they tragically helped to end his life and radically altered those of his wife, children, and extended family members.

Despite his death, Julio continues to "reside" in East Los Angeles, not far from the home of his family in Boyle Heights—in the very close-by city of Montebello where he is buried in the Resurrection Cemetery. The irony is that it took his death to make him an authorized "resident." In life, his existence in the United States was only partially welcomed at best by American society—largely as a laborer. In life, he always faced the threat of deportation. In death, however, he is allowed to stay.

This says a lot about the nature of a transnational entity such as what we might call Juchipila, MexUSA. It is one inescapably defined and scarred by the U.S.-Mexico boundary, and its associated practices that privilege the lives of some over others, and that ultimately deny the very humanity of many who make up that transnational space, bringing about untimely deaths and other forms of suffering in the process.

San Ysidro, California,
U.S.A. September 2005.
Protest against
launch of "Friends of the
Border Patrol."

ABOUT 175 PEOPLE CAME to Julio César Gallegos's funeral mass on August 20, 1998, at the Resurrection Church in Boyle Heights. People from the neighborhood, some of Jackie's coworkers, friends, and family from Inglewood and other parts of greater Los Angeles, and Juchipilans from all over California attended.

Press accounts painted a scene of sorrow at the church and cemetery: "Murillo [Jackie's last name], whose second child is due on Sept. 16, cried softly in the church's front row," one described. "Her 2-year-old son, Julio César Gallegos Jr., climbed into the arms of his grandmother, Maria Rodriguez [Jackie's mother]. Sitting nearby were Gallegos's father, Florentino Gallegos, who came from Mexico, and other relatives and friends."[1] Another reported: "At the coffin, Julio's father, Florentino, a former Mexican police officer, stood at [Jackie's] side, resolute and holding his head high until he broke down sobbing and bracing himself against his other son."[2] Published photos from the cemetery showed a distraught Jackie weeping over her husband's coffin.[3]

Apart from the moving descriptions, what was striking about the accounts of the funeral and, more broadly, analyses of the deaths of Julio and the migrants with whom he was traveling was how narrowly responsibility for the tragedy was framed. Echoing the federal gov-

167

ernment, many pointed the finger at the smugglers—the priest, himself an immigrant from Mexico, who celebrated the funeral mass, for example, referred to them as "murderers." Other analyses highlighted poverty in Mexico, or held Mexico's government partly responsible for not ensuring that people in Mexico have sufficient work and food to keep them there, and for not trying to stop migrants from crossing the boundary. One, an editorial in the *Imperial Valley Press*, assigned a share of the blame to people on "this side" for employing "illegal" migrants.[4]

As a whole, these analyses are more multifaceted than one frequently finds in public debate about such matters. Many in the society at-large, for instance, limit blame to the dead migrants themselves for breaking the law and for making what they see as a free choice to migrate despite the legal transgressions (and associated dangers) involved.[5] Some assign responsibility to the physical environment, suggesting that the harsh conditions of the borderlands were at fault— as if migrants' need to trek through the desert were an act of nature.[6] And mimicking official Washington, many limit blame to the *coyotes*. While many accounts express sympathy for migrants and actually assert that the enhanced boundary enforcement regime has funneled crossers into more arduous, risky terrain and led to an increase in deaths, what all these explanations share is what they do not discuss: by far the most important factor—that is, the very existence of U.S.-Mexico boundary as a line of exclusion, and the agents that produce, police, and champion it and the associated category of "illegal alien."

To state what should be obvious, if migrants were allowed to freely cross the divide—and, by extension, reside and work within the United States without fear of arrest and deportation due to immigration status—there would be no migrant deaths. That such a point is so rarely made speaks to how hegemonic, accepted, uncontroversial, "natural"—and thus invisible in terms of being an appropriate object of scrutiny—the boundary and its associated practices and identities have become (even among many migrants[7]). Thus, in the case of the editorial from the *Imperial Valley Press*, in response to the contention that the Border Patrol was responsible for the deaths for forcing migrants into the mountains and desert east of the San Diego area, it asserted that the agency "was only doing its job"—a job that is presumably beyond question. As for those who give the Border Patrol its job or have contributed to the rapid buildup of boundary enforcement that has taken place since the early 1990s, they were not even mentioned and, hence, not at all made responsible for what befalls unauthorized migrants. Thus, the enforcement and exclusion are presented as beyond question and matters for which no one should be scrutinized or criticized. Ten years after Julio's Cesar's death, the same narrow analysis, empty rhetoric, and hand-wringing pervade public discussion of migrant fatalities.

But more typically, the deaths bring about little to no reaction. To the extent that they are reported nationally, silence is the typical response. In many ways, migrant deaths have become a way of life in the U.S.-Mexico borderlands and, more broadly, in the intersections between "first" and "third" worlds.

In this sense, the boundary is one between life and death in that on what side one is born, and works and resides—or at least has a right to do so in the case of the unsanctioned migrant—profoundly shapes one's life circumstances, intensely informing to what resources and opportunities one has access. Those on the less privileged side of the social and geographical divide must endure a disproportionate share of the indignities, insecurities, and various manifestations of violence that make up a deeply unequal, unjust world order.

Deaths such as that of Julio César Gallegos are only the most extreme form of the indignities, insecurities, and violence. To the extent that they are visible to those on the more privileged side, the fatalities are seen as an unfortunate, seemingly unavoidable fact of life. And when referred to in establishment circles, or by those who want to defend or enhance the status quo, the deaths become a reason to further the divides between rich and poor, white and nonwhite, the so-called first and third worlds.

Take the case of 46-year-old Adela Hernandez. Her body was found in Sunland Park, New Mexico, just to the west of El Paso in July 2006. Her 13-year-old son, Julio Hernandez, had dragged his dead mother's body through the desert after she collapsed. According to the one newspaper report on her death, she appeared to have died of dehydration or exposure to heat. She and her son were from somewhere in central Mexico and were on their way to Florida where her husband and Julio's father worked.[8]

Like so many such reports, it elicited almost no public response. An exception was the Minuteman Civil Defense Corps, a self-described group of "citizen volunteers" who seek "to secure America's sovereign territory against incursion, invasion, and terrorism." They commented that it showed the danger of "open borders" while proclaiming, "Securing the border is the humane thing to do."[9]

In responding as they did, the Minutemen are not alone: many who champion ever-stronger levels of boundary and immigration enforcement now decry the deaths and use them to bolster immigration and boundary restrictionist positions. In the highly controversial "Sensenbrenner bill" that the House of Representatives passed in December 2005, there was a section called "Fencing and Other Border Security Improvements," for example; the first item it mentions in listing reasons for improved barriers along the boundary is this: "Hundreds of people die crossing our international border with Mexico every year."[10] Representative Duncan Hunter, a Republican from the San Diego area (later a candidate for the party's 2008 Republican nomination for the presidency), the individual most responsible for

the walls and fences that increasingly litter the border landscape—
some people refer to him as the "Secretary of da fence"—argued to
Bush administration officials in 2006 that more boundary barriers are
a good way to prevent deaths. "If you can save lives by fencing the
desert, why not fence the desert?" he asked.[11]

In addition to ignoring the fact that the very boundary militarization that they are demanding more of has led to the increase in
migrant deaths, such invocations of the defense of life exhibit a narrow conception of what life is. It is not simply biological existence.
In the case of Julio, he was attempting to rejoin his family, to return
to his home and job, and to realize a level of socioeconomic security
effectively denied to him in central Mexico—to live, in other words,
in the full sense of the word.

But such a view of life and security is not the one invoked in the
United States when matters of the boundary and migration are dis-
cussed. It is one limited to "us"—those of us who have a supposed
right to be here. That it more often than not does not include our
"illegal" and noncitizen neighbors and coworkers and people from
beyond U.S. territorial confines demonstrates that just as migrant
deaths have become a way of life in the U.S. borderlands, the boundary, and the violence, injustice, and exclusion that it embodies, has
become increasingly central to our very ways of thinking and seeing
the world. It is so embedded in mainstream thought that is highly difficult for us to see beyond it. Thus Democrats and Republicans
alike—from Hillary Clinton and Barack Obama to John McCain and
Mike Huckabee—champion ever more "security" along the boundary.[12] While they might differ on the height and length of additional
walls, fences, and vehicle barriers, or the number of additional Border Patrol agents, they share the assumption that the boundary is
insufficiently guarded and that more protection against would-be
threats is needed.

Nogales, Sonora, Mexico. October 2005. Annual border mobilization, organized by Derechos Humanos of Tucson and others, where marchers from Nogales, Arizona, converge with marchers from Nogales, Sonora, at the U.S.-Mexico boundary. Bottom photo: members of Danza Mexica Cuauhtemoc.

That quest for a particular form of security killed Julio César Gallegos. Since his death, literally thousands more migrants have perished trying to cross the U.S.-Mexico boundary. In this sense, Julio's death was hardly unique. While one can only understand the specific tragedy that befell him through the particulars of his case, the particulars can provide a very partial explanation at best. Given the huge death toll, systematic factors were clearly at work—and still are.

—◦◦◦—

"Security" in the United States is what some have referred to as a "God-word"—something universally embraced, and insufficiently questioned—at least among supporters of the status quo. Debate and polling within the country as a whole regarding the U.S.-Mexico boundary—especially since the September 11, 2001, Al Qaeda attacks—show that the vast majority of the U.S. population sees the international divide as a protector, and a necessary one, against external threats. In a world of growing "flows" of people, goods, and ideas across boundaries, so the thinking goes, the potential for threatening forces to enter national territory is greater than ever. In this spirit, Congressman Tom Tancredo of Colorado, a candidate for the 2008 Republican presidential nomination, stated in February 2006, "Yes, many who come across the [U.S.-Mexico] border are workers. But among them are people coming to kill you and me and your children."[13]

Hyperbolic analyses are hardly new. In the run-up to Operation Wetback in 1954, for instance, Democratic senator Hubert Humphrey characterized Mexico as a country "in almost a death struggle to keep out of Communist control" and argued that Communist agents might infiltrate the United States across the insufficiently guarded southern boundary. Meanwhile Edmund Brown, California's attorney general, likened the divide to a door "open for potential saboteurs and fifth columnists."[14]

Such rhetoric has a long history, one that goes back to the very first piece of immigration control legislation in the United States, the Alien Friends Act of 1798. In this regard, the novelty of post–9-11 boundary-related rhetoric lies not so much in its general substance, but in its specific forms. However, even in the case of terrorism—to say nothing about street crime—rhetoric linking it to highly racialized outsiders, U.S. territorial boundaries, and unauthorized migrants, long precedes 9-11. Regardless of the "race," ethnicity, and national origins of the particular targeted groups, all of them have been characterized as threatening, as populations that need to be guarded against, as the polar opposite of what is deemed to be the ideal American.

These analyses flow from and reinforce the assumption that the United States needs strong, heavily policed territorial boundaries to provide protection against these alleged threats. They also have provided the foundation for the massive boundary and migrant policing apparatus that now exists. The result of all this in terms of what have been presented as border-related security threats (i.e., drugs, crime, and terrorism) is highly questionable.

Never before has it been so difficult to cross the boundary or has the migrant policing apparatus been as big as it is. And never have as many "illegals" who have crossed from Mexico without authorization been present in the United States as there are today. This apparent contradiction speaks to the high number of people trying to enter the United States surreptitiously, the sheer length of the boundary, the challenges of policing the arduous landscape of the borderlands,[15] and the great persistence and resourcefulness of migrants and those who smuggle them.[16]

As for fighting terrorism, which is what the Border Patrol now says is one of its primary functions, as of 2007 there was no documented basis for any suggested link of terrorism with Mexico or with movement across the U.S.-Mexico boundary.[17] Nonetheless, fears of terrorists emanating from Mexican territory fuels much vacuous discussion in Congress and provides fodder for many press accounts that typically highlight Border Patrol apprehensions of non-Mexican migrants as supposed proof of the threat. As in the case of the broader "war on terror" and similar to the emptiness of claims that link growing immigration to higher crime rates,[18] political actors have grossly exaggerated the threat of terrorism as the lack of any attacks since 2001—despite a still permeable boundary—demonstrates. In response to those who would say that this "proves" that the security measures along the boundary are working, political scientist John Mueller writes in a 2006 article,

> Americans are told—often by the same people who had once predicted imminent attacks—that the absence of international terrorist strikes in the United States is owed to the protective measures so hastily and expensively put in place after 9/11. But there is a problem with this argument. True, there have been no terrorist incidents in the United States in the last five years. But nor were there any in the five years before the 9/11 attacks, at a time when the United States was doing much less to protect itself.[19]

The overstated nature of the boundary-related threat is demonstrated by the Department of Homeland Security's own statistics. While it bills itself as an agency whose main goal is to fight terrorism, the Department filed claims of terrorism against only 12 (0.0015%) of the 814,073 people that it charged in immigration courts between 2004 and 2006.[20] As has always been the case, the target of boundary and immigration enforcement is human beings born outside of U.S. territory. What changes over time are the labels attached to them—"Communist," "illegal," "criminal," and "terrorist" being among the most socially marginalizing—and the related ideological smokescreens used to legitimate their exclusion, one of the most powerful being "the law."

Invocations of the law as a justification for particular activities—especially in the United States, where the dominant view is one that it is a country with a deep devotion to the rule of law—has the effect of shutting down debate. That, combined with the state's power to mold the collective mind-set of its citizenry to distinguish between "right" and "wrong" (through "the law") and to perceive the country's boundaries as almost sacred, helps explain to a significant degree why "illegal" migration resonates so profoundly with the public at large. For the vast majority of Americans, the wrongness of unsanctioned migration and the need to prevent it are simply beyond question. The law and its defense becomes an end in and of itself.[21]

Yet, history (as well as the present) teaches us that what is the law and what is just are often not synonymous. As Marlon Brando, in his role as a human rights lawyer in apartheid-era South Africa in the 1989 film, *A Dry White Season*, tells a client, "Justice and law could be described as distant cousins, and here . . . they're not even on speaking terms." One could just as easily make the same observation about boundary and immigration enforcement in the United States—and elsewhere across the globe—given the foundational injustices embodied by the very making of the country's boundaries and their related practices of exclusion.

Yet few of us—even those who perceive national exclusion as unacceptable—are willing to publicly say so. In part, given the ideological and material weight of the boundary and enforcement apparatus, it is for reasons of fear—fear of social ostracism—as well as of a sense of powerlessness.

I speak from experience: I recall being on a train in the mid-1990s traveling from San Diego, where I had been conducting research on Operation Gatekeeper, to Los Angeles. At the station in Oceanside, about forty miles north of San Diego, Border Patrol agents boarded the train and began asking passengers about their citizenship status, and then proceeded to ask anyone who hesitated or whom they suspected of lying for identification. In the process, the agents arrested, handcuffed, and removed a number of Spanish-speaking individuals from the train. Watching this, I was outraged, but I felt paralyzed, and, as a result, said nothing. Across the aisle from me, however, was a man in a suit and tie who appeared to be in his late sixties or early seventies. He began yelling loudly at the agents, saying that what they were doing reminded him of what he had witnessed the Nazis doing to people as a youth in Europe. No, the Border Patrol agents were not taking the arrestees to concentration camps or to death chambers. But the federal agents were treating them as permanent outsiders, as less than fully human, as people with fewer rights because of first and foremost who they were, where they were from, a characteristic the migrants had no control over. It took someone who lived through the Nazi era to have the ability to perceive it for what it was, and the courage to speak out.

Typically the individuals on the frontline who carry out such exclusion justify what they do by referencing the law, or by explaining that they are simply doing their job. But sometimes these agents of the state actually articulate a perception of migrants that is as shocking and inhumane as their actions aimed at expelling them from U.S. territory. One Border Patrol agent spoke about why he enjoyed his job, asking rhetorically, "Where else do they pay you to drive around and go hunting?" Another stated, "It's the thrill of the hunt, without the kill."[22]

That so many fail to see the perverse nature of such rhetoric and, more importantly, of the underlying ideology of national exclusion, and continue to embrace the security-unauthorized migrant-boundary nexus speaks not only to the power of the international divide to shape our ways of seeing the world, but also the depth of societal fear of "foreigners"—especially those from low-income and nonwhite parts of the world. That migrants are constructed as geographically—in addition to sociopolitically—outside helps explain why fears about terrorists and criminals from abroad translate into a focus on territorial boundaries to a much greater extent than fears about purveyors of violence from within the United States.

Consider, for example, the case of Timothy McVeigh, who, on April 19, 1995, bombed the Alfred P. Murrah Federal Building in Oklahoma City, killing 167 people and injuring hundreds more. McVeigh was not from Oklahoma City, nor even from the state of Oklahoma. Indeed, he crossed state boundaries to commit his crime. Had such movement been restricted, it might have been more difficult for McVeigh to do what he did. Nonetheless, his horrific act did not result in any attempt to restrict movement across state boundaries within the United States. The reason why is clear: he was a U.S. citizen (and a native-born one) with the right to unimpeded travel across national territory. He was not an outsider. He was a white male and a military veteran. He was—in terms of the dominant perception of what an American looks like—one of "us." Thus, his crime did not involve a perceived geographical transgression even though movement across space was a key element of his act. Given this perception, territorial security—at least one conceived in any way similar to that applied along the U.S.-Mexico boundary—is not the response. In the case of threats, real or imagined, emanating from beyond U.S. boundaries, however, they are perceived as primarily territorial in nature and thus necessitate a response involving a buildup of physical boundaries. In other words, the territories from where these dangers come are seen as inherently threatening. It is hardly a coincidence that these areas happen to be places where wealth and income is significantly less than that accumulated in the United States and where the populations are largely nonwhite. In that regard, the divide and conflict is one between what is perceived by many as a civilized first world, made up of Western countries, and a barbaric third world, composed of the countries of Latin America, Africa, and most of Asia.

Antagonistic relationships between the so-called first and third worlds go back to the making of the modern world economy and nation-states. The conquest of what is today the U.S. Southwest, the dispossession and decimation of the indigenous population, and the settlement of the area by the conquering power was part of this process. And like all single events, it was unique. But it was also a manifestation of a much larger process of violence, slaughter, dispos-

Washington Heights, Manhattan, New York, U.S.A. March 2006. Protest against proposed immigration legislation (HR 4437—the so-called Sensenbrenner bill).

session, and theft, one that began with the rise of European imperialism in the sixteenth century. At that time, levels of socioeconomic development across the world were generally equal. In fact in terms of political-economic development, Europe was in many key ways behind China, what is today Pakistan and northern India, and parts of West Africa, among other regions. In five short centuries, however, there has been a radical reworking of the global economy, resulting in the creation of great wealth for some, a mixed bag for most, and outright misery for many.[23]

—✳—

Maintaining an unjust world order requires work, one that enshrines the type of double standards that form the foundation of a world order in which processes of racism and its internationally institutionalized cousin, nation-statism, are inextricably intertwined. In August 2004, some articles in the *New York Times* showed just how all this functions—and the simultaneously deadly and enlivening effects these processes have.

In a lead article entitled, "In Pursuit of Fabulousness" in the newspaper's "Escapes" section, the *Times* introduced its readership to the place where Mikhail Baryshnikov, the ballet star, has his vacation home. It is located close to the sprawling Southern Greek Revival beachside abode of his good friend and local native son, Oscar de la Renta, in the same town where the fashion designer and singer Julio Iglesias are partners in a luxury resort and club. Prices there range from $310,000 for a three-bedroom villa away from the sea to several millions dollar for property on the beach—such as Iglesias's home, a six-acre Balinese compound.

The place is "the new St. Bart's," a reference to Saint-Barthélemy, the tiny Caribbean island in the French West Indies that serves as a lavish get-away destination for many of the global rich and famous. This "new" St. Bart's, however, is better than the real one in so many ways according to the article. In addition to having more favorable prices, "it's so close," explains Margarita Waxman—only three and a half hours by plane from New York City. The SoHo resident, just retired from a public relations job at the upscale jeweler Bulgari, flies back and forth monthly.[24] She had recently paid $3 million for four acres of beachfront for a new villa there, instead of in the harder-to-get-to St. Bart's, where she has often vacationed.

"There's so much building going on," gushes Amelia Vicini, a fashion editor at *Town & Country* magazine, who was born and raised in the tropical paradise. "Every time I go home, I am amazed. The winter season is crazy, full of people—celebrities, A-listers, everyone."

This hot location is the Dominican Republic, a half-island nation (the other half of the island of Hispaniola being Haiti). "Until a few years ago, the Dominican Republic had a reputation as second-rate, and affluent shoppers for second homes largely stayed away," the *Times* explained. "Then, in the early '90s, developers . . . began attracting attention with luxurious gated communities on the water."[25]

Only one day earlier, the *Times* had run an Associated Press article on the inside of the newspaper's main section about a different type of water-related escape involving the Dominican Republic. Entitled "Dominicans Saved from Sea Tell of Attacks and Deaths of Thirst," the piece recounted the horrific experiences of about eighty Dominican migrants fleeing the poverty in their homeland. Having paid $450 each—about a year's income for most Dominicans—they tried to sail clandestinely to Puerto Rico so that they would be then able to fly to the U.S. mainland free of immigration controls.

The engine of the small wooden boat died two days after the July 29 departure from the coastal village of Limón. By the next day, the vessel's water and meager food supply—chocolate, peanuts, sardines, and some coconuts—were depleted. The passengers began to panic.

Two lactating women reportedly dripped their breast milk into a bottle for passengers to drink. Another told of eating his tube of Colgate to survive. The boat drifted at sea for almost two weeks. People began dying on the fifth day, their bodies thrown overboard into shark-infested waters by those still living. Many jumped overboard in desperation and drowned. Forty-seven ended up perishing on the voyage. Another eight died of dehydration after Dominican authorities rescued a total of thirty-nine people.[26]

In a follow-up article on August 16, the *Times* described the homes of the majority of the inhabitants of one of the villages of many of the migrants as being made of "lashed-together pieces of tin." Attempts to

New York, New York, U.S.A. March 2006. Angela holding photo of brother at children's vigil against deportation organized by Families for Freedom. An Iraq War veteran, Warren was then being held in detention under deportation proceedings. He has since been released.

flee from such poverty to a better life in the United States had increased over the preceding year in the context of a severe economic downturn in the Dominican Republic. In the previous ten months alone, U.S. authorities had arrested more than 7,000 Dominican crossers, and thousands more had surely evaded the web of enforcement.[27]

Such unauthorized crossings have a long and deep history given the intense migratory ties between the United States and the Dominican Republic.[28] And so do migrant deaths. A 1998 report in the *Los Angeles Times*, for example, spoke of "human bones littering the small shoals and islets between the Dominican and Puerto Rican shores" as a result of crossing-related fatalities.[29] In November 2003, the U.S. Border Patrol estimated that nearly 300 people had either died or vanished—undoubtedly an undercount—while crossing the Mona Passage between the Dominican Republic and Puerto Rico over the previous three years. And another 164 U.S.-bound migrants had reportedly died or disappeared elsewhere in the Caribbean.[30]

In the late 1990s, the economy of the Dominican Republic was growing at a fast pace. But the economic expansion did little for the poor and middle class, many members of which also were attempting to make the perilous journey. By 2004, that expansion had disappeared. Unemployment stood officially at 16 percent, and the rate of inflation was 32 percent. Meanwhile, the Dominican peso had lost half of its value against the U.S. dollar over the previous two years, resulting in a doubling of prices during that period. Saddled with a $6 billion debt and under heavy pressure from the International Monetary Fund via a $600-million loan agreement, the government in Santo Domingo was promising austerity measures, ones that would presumably lead to cuts in social services and government jobs and a reduction in subsidies for basic necessities, which, barring an economic upturn, would surely fuel pressures for out-migration. In addition, the country's electrical system was a mess. The government privatized generating plants in the 1990s with the goal of lessening blackouts. The situation had worsened, however, as electricity was typically only available for a few hours a day.[31]

Little of this profoundly affects the lives of rich Dominicans or the affluent foreigners eagerly buying up the country's prime beachfront property. As an envious real estate agent from St. Bart's explains, "You can be a king in the Dominican for very little money." Or, as Margarita Waxman effuses, "There's a quaintness about it. It has all the beauty of St. Bart's, only more bohemian."[32]

If, as Stuart Hall and Ruth Wilson Gilmore contend,[33] racism is the fatal coupling of power and difference—fatal in the sense that it shapes one's life (and death) circumstances—the reporting on the Dominican Republic in the *New York Times* exposes (albeit unintentionally) the true face of what many have called global apartheid.[34] It is one in which the relatively rich and largely white of the world are generally free to travel and live wherever they would like and to access the resources they "need." Meanwhile the relatively poor and largely nonwhite are typically forced to subsist in places where there are not enough resources to provide sufficient livelihood or, in order to overcome their deprivation and insecurity, to risk their lives trying to overcome ever-stronger boundary controls put into place by rich countries that reject them.

Apartheid might seem like an inappropriate metaphor to employ given the fact that there is no legally enshrined racial segregation between the so-called first and third worlds, and that there are many third-world-origin peoples who have citizenship, and live and work in countries throughout the West. Although discrimination in terms of who is allowed to enter and reside in a particular country regularly occurs, national governments determine who can enter a country first and foremost on the basis of the would-be immigrant's national citizenship and socio-economic situation, a form of discrimination seen as fully legitimate in international affairs. Nonetheless, if we move beyond the question of what are the specific motivations that under-lie the system of immigration regulation and the particular mechanisms that are associated with it, and instead focus on effects and outcomes, there is little question that immigration enforcement in countries such as the United States or those of the European Union functions in an apartheid-like manner. No, it does not achieve "per-fect" separation, but neither did South Africa. The idea of apartheid embraced by its champions there was never fully realized—nor could it have been. Indeed, the production and maintenance of the privilege enjoyed by white South Africans necessitated interaction with non-whites—in a highly exploitative manner. As Lindsay Bremner writes,

> While black and white bodies were, in theory, assigned to certain localities, fixed in space, in point of fact they were caught up in continuous circulatory migrations and asym-metrical intimacies. Black bodies were needed to nurse white children, to clean white houses, and to labor in white indus-try, to work on white mines. White bodies policed, regulated, and administered black space. Bodies moved through and interacted with each other's space on a daily basis.[35]

In other words, interaction and mixing occurred but because it was necessitated to a significant degree by white South African society. Resistance by blacks and others to the legally enshrined segregation also undermined the proclaimed goal of purity. But the fact that there was a gap between the rhetoric and the reality does not alter the fact that apartheid, by allowing unequal access to and influence over the country's socio-political-economic resources and processes on the basis of who allegedly belonged and who did not, reflected and repro-duced profoundly different life and death experiences for white and

nonwhite South Africans as a whole, differential outcomes legiti-
mated on the basis of geographic origin and ancestry.

Strikingly similar is the gap between the "ideal" of separate, sovereign nation-states and the reality of messy and racialized
boundary-crossings based on systemic relations of domination and
subordination between the West and the rest of the world. They are
also similar in that nonwhite spaces outside of the West become the
venues to pursue vices prohibited or difficult to pursue in predomi-
nantly white ones. Just as Sun City, the casino resort area in the
nominally independent "homeland" of Bophuthatswana, served as a
hospitable locale for gambling and topless female revues in apartheid-
era South Africa, so, too, do many "third world" destinations today
serve as the vice-ridden playgrounds for "first world" travelers seeking escapist pleasures at relatively low cost. Mexican border towns
played a similar role in the era of Prohibition and continue to do so
today (albeit far less than in the past).

In a world of profound inequality, there are few if any nations that
share a land boundary with the level of disparity as wide as that
between Mexico and the United States. Which side of a boundary
one is born on—something that is permanent and that one cannot
change—profoundly shapes the resources to which one has access,
the amount of political power on the international stage one has,
where one can go, and thus how one lives and dies. This is the
essence of racism as it allows for double standards based on the
assumption that some should have greater rights because of their geographic origins or ancestry. And given the unjust nature of the global
political economy, which embodies this unequal allocation of rights
and which national governments enforce, these double standards are
also the essence of nation-statism as well.

Julio César Gallegos's death and the fatalities of countless other unauthorized boundary crossers are produced at the intersection of processes of globalization and nationalization. Relatively few enjoy a highly disproportionate share of the benefits of this globalization, a manifestation of the deep socioeconomic inequality that plagues the contemporary world. Boundary enforcement—a manifestation of nationalization—is part of an effort to maintain and reproduce that inequality.

Events in 1986 show the contradictions and complementarities of these processes that are seemingly at odds. That year, Congress passed the Immigration Reform and Control Act, known by its acronym, IRCA, resulting in the authorization of a 50 percent increase in INS enforcement budget.[36] Although it is not clear that such authorization of resources resulted in a significant expansion of the INS enforcement capacity in the short term,[37] it did strengthen the foundation needed for future growth. Also in 1986, Mexico entered the General Agreement on Tariffs and Trade, a manifestation of the embrace of that country's ruling class of a liberalized national political economy—a move very much supported and encouraged by the United States. These two developments marked an intensification and public acknowledgment of what had long been Washington's de facto boundary policy: one that championed growing economic integration between the United States and Mexico while endeavoring to achieve greater levels of control over transboundary labor migration.[38] Similarly, 1994 was the year that the North American Free Trade Agreement went into effect and that Operation Gatekeeper began.[39]

In a number of ways, these seemingly countervailing developments speak to the tensions inherent in a global political order dominated by nation-states, and a world economic system that pays far less heed to national sovereignty. But they also demonstrate the profound cynicism and hypocrisy that maintenance of an unjust global order entails.

Take the following cases, for example. Bernard Kerik was George W. Bush's nominee in 2004 to head the Department of Homeland Security, and thus to take charge of boundary and immigration enforcement. (In 2003, the INS was disbanded, and the Border Patrol became part of Customs and Border Protection in the newly created Department of Homeland Security.) But numerous ethical and legal problems—among them Kerik's employment of an undocumented migrant as his family's nanny—derailed his nomination. Similarly, President Bill Clinton's first nominee for attorney general, Zoë Baird, became untenable when it came to light in 1993 that she had hired two undocumented Peruvian migrants as domestic servants. About eight years later, Bush's candidate for secretary of labor, conservative activist Linda Chavez, withdrew her nomination after it became known that she had provided housing and money to an "illegal" immigrant from Guatemala, who, in return for what Chavez called acts of charity, performed various household tasks. Ironically, Chavez had been critical of Baird in 1993 for her employment transgressions.[40] And prior to successfully playing the immigration- and boundary-crisis cards to energize his flagging reelection campaign in the early 1990s, Pete Wilson had had a very different relationship to unauthorized migrants and boundary control. In 1983, while in the U.S. Senate, he coauthored legislation that prohibited immigration authorities from raiding farms without a judge's warrant. This became federal law in 1986 and effectively put a halt to farm inspections, thus sheltering unauthorized workers (and their employers) from arrest. On numerous occasions, Wilson also pressured U.S. officials to stop workplace raids on California companies. And in the late 1970s, he and his wife employed an unauthorized migrant as their maid.[41]

Such matters illustrate how globalization—in the form of flows of people and goods across boundaries—both undermines migrant and boundary policing and, in a profoundly unequal world politically governed by a nation-state logic that demands exclusion, necessitates such regulation. For the most privileged classes, national territorial boundary making is, among other things, a game, one played cynically when it suits their interests. For those at the global political-geographical and socioeconomic margins, by contrast, it can be a life-and-death matter. It is one that plays out not only at the boundary itself but also in places on either side of the line, one that separates and brings together those places and shapes them in the process.

—◦◦◦—

Olivia Luna Noguera tried unsuccessfully to overcome the territorial boundaries of the contemporary world order. In late July 2006, the 11-year-old was found on the land of the Tohono O'odham Nation in southern Arizona. She was wearing pink sneakers and was unconscious. Efforts to revive her failed. She died of cardiac arrest brought about by hyperthermia. Her body temperature was 106 degrees. Accompanied by her 17-year-old sister, Marisol, she was trying to get to Atlanta, Georgia, to reunite with her parents.

In a world of intensifying ties that transcend international boundaries, and great instability and insecurity, one brought about to a significant degree by the violence of U.S. foreign policy and by neoliberal trade policies that undermine people's livelihoods, many will no doubt continue to try to cross the U.S.-Mexico boundary despite the risks. This is true regardless of the number of Border Patrol agents and the length and height of the proposed walls. As one man who was getting ready to try to cross into Arizona told a reporter just two days before Olivia perished, "Our needs are greater than our fears."[42]

Such needs most likely brought Olivia's parents to Atlanta, so they could provide for their children. And such needs undoubtedly drove them to try to reunite with their daughters—a basic "family value"

Buenos Aires National Wildlife Refuge, Arizona, U.S.A. June 2005. The third annual Migrant Trail—a 75-mile journey from Sásabe, Sonora, to Tucson, Arizona, where participants walk in solidarity with their migrant sisters and brothers who have walked this trail and others, and lost their lives.

lost in what passes for debate among those championing a further enforcement buildup along the boundary.

Many will no doubt point their fingers at Olivia's mother and father, asking what type of parents would expose their 11-year-old daughter to such a dangerous trip. But such blame is misplaced. Instead, one should ask what type of people would compel the parents to make a risky choice by denying them and their children the right to be united and to work and reside where they can have access to resources needed for a life of well-being.

Such cases expose the violence inherent in immigration and boundary policing. It is violent in that it denies people some of their most basic rights—a right to life, a right to be free from inhuman or degrading treatment, a right to a standard of living adequate for the health and well-being of oneself and one's family, and a right to work and have just and favorable conditions for such. It is violent in that the boundary as it now exists denies people the right to access the resources they need to realize those rights—rights contained within the Universal Declaration of Human Rights and other international covenants.[43]

Deaths and other forms of violence are not unique to the United States–Mexico boundary. Migrant fatalities occur regularly along the geographical margins of Europe and along the boundary between South Africa and Zimbabwe[44]—just to give a couple of examples. A 2006 issue of the *First Post*, an online daily magazine, carried images that shockingly demonstrate such insecurity. They included one of an exhausted migrant—presumably from somewhere in Africa—crawling onto a beach of Spain's Canary Islands (off the coast of Western Sahara and Morocco) while three sunbathers look on from a distance. The photo captures brilliantly and painfully the unequal access to particular nationalized spaces experienced by people across the globe.[45] For those sitting on the beach witnessing the migrant, arriving at the tropical sands was most likely a relatively easy experience—even if they were from a country other than Spain—because of their socioeconomic status and other geographically informed privileges (one of which relates to their ability to move across global space). For the migrant, trying to reach the Canary Islands by traversing the treacherous waters of the Atlantic was literally a death-defying activity as the heavy migrant death toll in the Canaries demonstrates. One estimate (from the Canary Islands vice-director of immigration) contends that upward of 6,000 migrants died trying to get to the Spanish archipelago—one out of every six that successfully reached the islands—in 2006 alone.[46] Such violence is inherent to varying extents in all international boundaries. But it is along the boundaries between rich and poor, the haves and have-nots, where the violence—and the insecurity—are most pronounced.

There are alternatives to this state of affairs. Given that international migration is often the result of the breakdown of political, economic, and social systems, as well as institutionalized injustice, we need to work at home and abroad in solidarity with those who suffer the consequences of such instability to redress this phenomena—especially to the extent that the policies and practices of the rich and powerful in countries such as the United States help bring them about. This would prove to be a far more humane and effective method for addressing the myriad factors that lead people to migrate than continuing to fortify the territorial and sociopolitical boundaries between "us" and "them." Beyond commitments incurred by historical injustices and concrete social ties, there are even larger ethical and political obligations.[47] Given the gross socioeconomic disparities and associated insecurity that plague many countries, international freedom of movement is an absolute necessity from a social justice and a human rights perspective.[48] While allowing freedom of movement and residence will not by itself eliminate the injustices of the contemporary global order— just as the end of legal apartheid in South Africa has not led to the end to that society's deep race and class disparities—it will at least permit people increased opportunities to realize livelihoods of dignity and, on a collective level, to organize to combat injustices with full civil and human rights.

—~~~—

On July 22, 2002, Jackie, Andrew, Julio Jr., Doña Maria (Jackie's mother), and Tino (Julio César's older brother)—along with other members of their extended family—drove down to Tijuana, to the

Benjamin Hill, Sonora, Mexico. June 2006. Thousands of migrants, many from Central America, risk life and limb by train hopping through Mexico to reach the U.S.-Mexico border (see Evans 2006). Here, Alfredo continues his journey northward.

section of the boundary wall that serves as a memorial to the lack of international freedom of movement. On it are hundreds of crosses with the names, birthplaces, and ages of migrants who have died in California since the mid-1990s while trying to enter the United States. Catholic priests, one from Brazil and another from Mexico, and volunteers associated with Tijuana's Casa del Migrante, a migrant shelter, were also present. The multinational gathering was there to remember Julio—about four years after he left Tijuana for Mexicali. On the wall, was a new cross, one with his name.

Jackie cried as she thanked all those in attendance for coming. After the ceremony, the volunteers from Casa del Migrante paid their respects to the family. The first one, a young woman, embraced Jackie, telling her that she had lost her father to the boundary only two years earlier.

"I always feared that people would forget him," his brother Tino admitted after a brief, but very moving ceremony. "Now I know that he is remembered." "It's so beautiful," Jackie said afterward in reference to all the crosses, "that these people have made this memorial."

Jackie watched as Tino played with her sons, picking each of them up and throwing them in the air as they squealed with delight. Her look was one of happiness and sorrow. "I wish they had a father to do such things with them."

Andrew—not even four at the time—had little idea why he was there. Julio Jr., then in the first grade, remembers his father and still today frequently invokes him. He already knew how to read when the ceremony took place. When he saw the words "Julio César Gallegos" on the cross, he asked his mother, "Is my daddy here?"

—◈—

Tijuana, Baja California, Mexico. July 2002. Memorial for Julio.

About one year before Julio César Gallegos died in the Imperial Valley, on July 4, 1997, I watched a rally calling for a crackdown on unwanted immigration and for increased militarization of the boundary outside the Westwood Federal Building in Los Angeles. There I saw a woman carrying a sign that read, "1848: You lost, we won. Get over it."[49]

The sign was a powerful reminder of the enduring legacy of the U.S.-Mexico War—as well as the so-called Indian wars that surrounded it[50]—a conflict that involved a large number of killings and widespread dispossession of the indigenous and Mexican populations. What was taken away was not only land but, for those now cut off from the territory to which they previously had access, all the rights that go along with it, like the right to move, live, and work within. And for those members of the conquered populations caught within the boundaries of the expanding United States or who would subsequently migrate to it, their rights in their new country would prove to be conditional and restricted. The theft was an inextricable part of the process to Americanize what is now the U.S. Southwest.

Typically, people do not quietly accept such gross injustice. They make efforts to get back what is, or should be, theirs. Thus, the original violence that created the injustice, what one might call a violence of foundation, normally necessitates efforts to maintain the spoils of treachery—a violence of conservation, in the words of historian Arno Mayer.[51] In this sense, the sign also demonstrates how the violence that the war embodied and produced lives on.

One of the tricks required in moving from a violence of foundation to one of conservation is to erase the original violence from our collective memory and thus normalize what has been stolen, to make seem just what is unjust. Through this, the violence of conservation becomes legitimized and, to most, invisible as violence (if it is even known). Thus, today, to suggest that violence and the very making of the United States—and, by extension, its territorial boundaries—have, from the beginning, gone hand in hand,[52] is to run the risk of ridicule or worse. This explains how and why the U.S-Mexico boundary has effectively become a burial site of history and geography, one of the more powerful manifestations of what writer Gore Vidal has referred to as the United States of Amnesia.[53]

The sign, moreover, was a reminder of just how strong—and contentious and divisive—attachments to places, especially national ones, often are. While people and places are dynamically interrelated by flows and connections that transcend boundaries, power is always present in the movement and flows across them, affecting individuals and social groups in unequal ways. As geographer Doreen Massey writes about the relationship between social power and mobility within and between places, "some are more in charge of it than others; some initiate flows and movement, others don't; some are more on the receiving end of it than others; some are effectively imprisoned by it."[54]

To break out of this metaphorical prison requires that we treat places and boundaries, and the people associated with them, as dynamic, fluid—as connected. It was this message that some graffiti that I first saw in 2006 on the Mexican side of boundary wall that runs between Nogales, Arizona, and Nogales, Sonora, was trying to communicate. It said in Spanish something to the effect, "If you turn this wall on its side, it becomes a bridge."

As long as there is a United States of America, there will be territorial and social boundaries between it and the rest of the world. What is not given is the nature of those boundaries. Whether they are walls or bridges, or boundaries of death or of life, whether we perceive and treat those on the other side of those boundaries as inferior and less worthy of lives of multifaceted security, or as fully human and thus deserving of the same rights and privileges as us, is, as always, a matter up for grabs.

Within the United States, and across the globe, there are organizations and movements fighting to tear down walls and build bridges between places and people. They, along with migrants who live their very lives beyond boundaries and struggle for a more just world,[55] point to the direction in which we must head.

Tijuana, Baja California Norte, Mexico. November 2001. ¿Cuantos Mas? "How Many More?" As of late 2007, the number of migrant bodies recovered in the U.S.-Mexico borderlands since 1995 totaled more than 4,000.

Boyle Heights, Los Angeles, California, U.S.A. November 2007. (Clockwise from top left) Jackie, Doña Maria, Andrew, and Julio Jr.

APPENDIX A

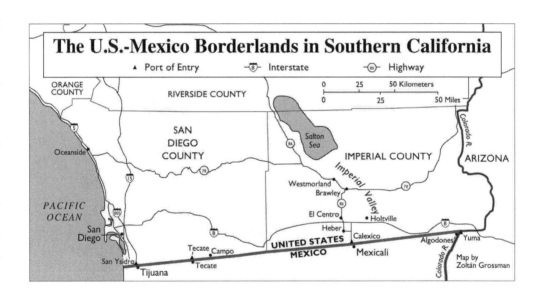

The U.S.-Mexico Borderlands in Southern California

Map by Zoltán Grossman

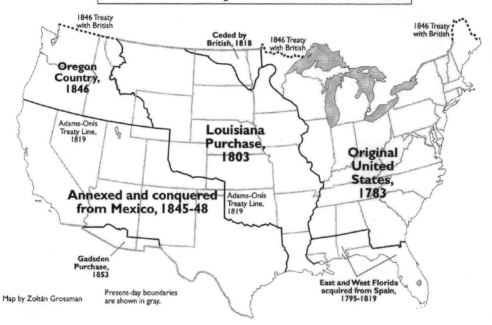

The Territorial Expansion of the United States

Map by Zoltán Grossman

Present-day boundaries are shown in gray.

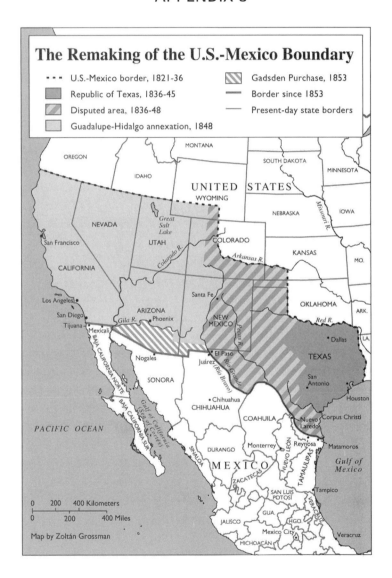

The Remaking of the U.S.-Mexico Boundary

- ▪ ▪ ▪ U.S.-Mexico border, 1821-36
- Republic of Texas, 1836-45
- Disputed area, 1836-48
- Guadalupe-Hidalgo annexation, 1848
- Gadsden Purchase, 1853
- Border since 1853
- Present-day state borders

Map by Zoltán Grossman

APPENDIX D

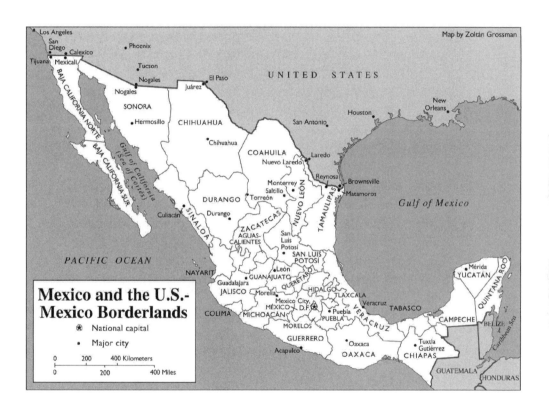

Mexico and the U.S.-Mexico Borderlands

⊛ National capital

• Major city

Map by Zoltán Grossman

BIBLIOGRAPHY

Acuña, Rodolfo. *A Community under Siege: A Chronicle of Chicanos East of the Los Angeles River, 1945–1975.* Los Angeles: Chicano Studies Research Center, University of California, Los Angeles, 1984.

———. *Occupied America: A History of Chicanos.* New York: Harper Collins Publishers, 1988.

———. *Anything but Mexican: Chicanos in Contemporary Los Angeles,* New York: Verso, 1996.

Agence France Press. "Human Smugglers Launch 'Coyote Express' into US." May 18, 2007.

Aizenman, N.C. "Meeting Danger Well South of the Border." *Washington Post,* July 8, 2006: A1.

Alarcón, Rafael. "The Development of Hometown Associations in the United States and the Use of Social Remittances in Mexico." In *Sending Money Home: Hispanic Remittances and Community Development,* edited by Rodolfo O. de la Garza and Briant Lindsay Lowell, 101–124. Lanham, Md.: Rowman and Littlefield, 2002.

Allegro, Linda G. "Deportations in an Age of Neoliberalism." *AmeriQuests* 3, no. 1 (2006), http://ejournals.library.vanderbilt.edu/ameriquests/viewarticle.php?id=50.

Almaguer, Tomás. *Racial Fault Lines: The Historical Origins of White Supremacy in California.* Berkeley and Los Angeles: University of California Press, 1994.

Althaus, Dudley. "Dominican Migrants Sacrifice for Better Life in Puerto Rico." *Houston Chronicle,* November 2, 2003.

Alvarez, Lizette. "Fear and Hope in Immigrant's Furtive Existence." *New York Times,* December 20, 2006.

Andreas, Peter. *Border Games: Policing the U.S.-Mexico Divide.* Ithaca: Cornell University Press, 2000.

Annerino, John. *Dead in Their Tracks: Crossing America's Borderlands.* New York: Four Walls Eight Windows, 1999.

Arreola, Daniel D., and James R. Curtis. *The Mexican Border Cities: Landscape Anatomy and Place Personality*. Tucson: University of Arizona Press, 1993.

Associated Press, "Víctimas del desierto iban a Nueva York y LA," *La Opinión* (Los Angeles), August 18, 1998a.

———. "Bodies of Smugglers Found Among Illegal Immigrants Who Died in Desert." *Los Angeles Times*, August 19, 1998b.

———. "Cemetery Final Resting Place for Unidentified Immigrants Who Died Crossing." *Holland Sentinel* (Holland, Mich.), May 29, 2001, http://www.hollandsentinel.com/stories/052901/new_0529010005.shtml.

———. "Dominicans Saved from Sea Tell of Attacks and Deaths of Thirst." *New York Times*, August 12, 2004.

———. "Remittances to Mexico Increase 23 Percent in First Half of 2006," August 25, 2006.

———. "Mom: Missing Mentally Disabled Son, Illegally Deported." CNN.com, June 17, 2007.

Aubry Kaplan, Erin. "Welcome to Inglewood—Leave Your Aspirations Behind." *LA Weekly*, July 22–28, 2005.

Azuela, Mariano. *The Underdogs: A Novel of the Mexican Revolution*. Translated by E. Munguía, Jr. New York: Signet, 1963.

Bachelet, Pablo. "Study: Outlook Bleak for Migrants." McClatchy Newspapers, August 8, 2007.

Bacon, David. *The Children of NAFTA: Labor Wars on the U.S./Mexico Border*. Berkeley, Los Angeles, and London: University of California Press, 2004.

———. "Communities Without Borders." *Nation*, October 24, 2005.

———. *Communities Without Borders: Images and Voices from the World of Migration*. Ithaca, New York: Cornell University Press, 2007a.

———. "Time for a More Radical Immigrant Rights Movement." *American Prospect*, July 24, 2007b.

Bailey, Stanley R., Karl Eschbach, Jaqueline Maria Hagan, and Nestor Rodriguez. "Migrant Deaths at the Texas–Mexico Border, 1985–1994." Center for Immigration Research, University of Houston, January 1996.

Balderrama, Francisco E., and Raymond Rodríguez. *Decade of Betrayal: Mexican Repatriation in the 1930s*. Albuquerque: University of New Mexico Press, 1995.

Banks, Sandy. "Inglewood High Class of 1975: A Painful Lesson in Division." *Los Angeles Times*, August 28, 2005.

———. "Black Firefighter Settles Suit over Racial Prank." *Los Angeles Times*, November 9, 2006.

Bardacke, Frank. Telephone interview with author on June 28, 2006.

Barnes, Fred. "Crime Scene: Republicans with a Cause." *New Republic*, September 5, 1994: 30+.

Batalova, Jeanne. "Mexican Born Persons in the US Civilian Labor Force," *Immigration Facts* (Migration Policy Institute), no. 14, November 2006, http://www.migrationpolicy.org/pubs/FS14_MexicanWorkers2006.pdf.

Becerra, Hector. "Turf War Stops at the ER." *Los Angeles Times*, May 4, 2007.

Becerra, Hector, Rich Connell and Robert J. Lopez. "Business, but Not as Usual." *Los Angeles Times*, June 18, 2006.

Berestein, Leslie. "Immigration Protest Heads to D.C." *San Diego Union-Tribune*, February 3, 2006.

Berestein, Leslie and Diane Lindquist. "Dwindling Work Force Puts Pressure on Growers." *San Diego Union-Tribune*, June 27, 2007.

Bernstein, Nina. "A Mother Deported, and a Child Left Behind." *New York Times*, November 24, 2004.

———. "Caught Between Parents and the Law." *New York Times*, February 17, 2005.

Binder, Norman E., J. L. Polinard, and Robert D. Winkle. "Mexican American and Anglo Attitudes toward Immigration Reform: A View from the Border." *Social Science Quartely* 78, no. 2 (June 1997): 324–337.

Blackhawk, Ned. *Violence over the Land: Indians and Empires in the Early American West*. Cambridge, Mass.: Harvard University Press, 2006.

Bokovoy, Matthew F. "Inventing Agriculture in Southern California." *Journal of San Diego History* 45, no. 2 (Spring 1999), http://www.sandiegohistory.org/journal/ 99spring/agriculture.htm.

Bonacich, Edna, and Robert F. Goodman. *Deadlock in School Desegregation: A Case Study of Inglewood, California*. New York: Praeger Publishers, 1972.

Booker, Salih, and William Minter. "Global Apartheid." *Nation*, July 9, 2001.

"The Border Patrol" (editorial). *Imperial Valley Press*, circa September 24, 1927: 4.

Bremner, Lindsay. "Border/Skin." In *Against the Wall: Israel's Barrier to Peace*, edited by Michael Sorkin, 112–137. New York: New Press, 2005.

Brofenbrenner, Kate. 2000. "Uneasy Terrain: The Impact of Capital Mobility on Workers, Wages, and Union Organizing." Report submitted to the U.S. Trade Deficit Review Commission (September 6, 2000), http://digitalcommons.ilr.cornell.edu/reports/1.

Brown, Jim. *Riding the Line: The United States Customs Service in San Diego, 1885–1930*. Washington, D.C.: Department of the Treasury, United States Customs Service, 1991.

Buffington, Robert. "Prohibition in the Borderlands: National Government-Border Community Relations." *Pacific Historical Review* 63, no. 1 (February 1994): 19–38.

Bustillo, Miguel. "Border Agents: 'We're Never Going to Stop Them, Never.'" *Los Angeles Times*, August 13, 2006.

Burawoy, Michael. "The Functions and Reproduction of Migrant Labor: Comparative Material from Southern Africa and the United States." *American Journal of Sociology* 81, no. 5 (March 1976): 1050–87.

CCBRES Bulletin (published by the California Center for Border and Regional Economic Studies, San Diego State University, Imperial Valley Campus, Calexico), various issues.

Calavita, Kitty. *Inside the State: The Bracero Program, Immigration, and the I.N.S.* New York and London: Routledge, 1992.

———. "U.S. Immigration and Policy Responses: The Limits of Legislation." In *Controlling Immigration: A Global Perspective*, edited by Wayne Cornelius et al., 54–82. Stanford, Calif.: Stanford University Press, 1994.

Cañas, Jesus, Roberto Coronado and Robert W. Gilmer. "U.S., Mexico Deepen Economic Ties." *Southwest Economy* (January/February 2006); available online at http://dallasfed.org/research/swe/2006/swe0601c.html.

Cardenas, Gilbert. "Critical Issues in Using Government Data Collected Primarily for Non-Research Purposes." In *Quantitative Data and Immigration Research*, edited by Stephen R. Crouch and Roy Simón Bryce-Laporte, 55–98. Washington, D.C.: Research Institute on Immigration and Ethnic Studies, Smithsonian Institution, 1979.

Carens, Joseph H. "Reconsidering Open Borders: A Reply to Meilander." *International Migration Review* 33, no. 4 (1999): 1082–97.

———. "Open Borders and Liberal Limits: A Response to Isbister." *International Migration Review* 34, no. 2 (2000): 636–43.

Castillo, Guadalupe and Margo Cowan, eds. *It Is Not Our Fault: The Case for Amending Present Nationality Law to Make All Members of the Tohono O'odham Nation United States Citizens, Now and Forever.* Sells, Arizona: Tohono O'odham Nation, 2001.

Chang, Grace. *Disposable Domestics: Immigrant Women Workers in the Global Economy.* Cambridge, Mass.: South End Press, 2000.

Chapman, Leonard F. "Illegal Aliens: Time to Call a Halt!" *Reader's Digest*, October 1976: 188–192.

Chey, Elizabeth. "A City Where Bilingual Says Dual, Not Duel." *Orange County Register*, May 29, 1998.

Cockcroft, James D. *Outlaws in the Promised Land: Mexican Immigrant Workers and America's Future*. New York: Grove Press, 1986.

Coleman, Mathew. "Immigration Geopolitics beyond the Mexico-US Border." *Antipode* 39, no. 1 (2007): 54–76.

Cook, Melissa. "Banished for Minor Crimes: The Aggravated Felony Provision of the Immigration and Nationality Act as a Human Rights Violation." *Boston College Third World Law Journal* 23, no. 2 (2003): 293–330.

Cooper, Marc. "Showdown on Immigration." *Nation*, April 3, 2006.

———. "Lockdown in Greeley." *Nation*, February 26, 2007a.

———. "East Versus West." *LA Weekly*, May 2, 2007b.

Conniff, Ruth. "The War on Aliens." *Progressive*, October 22, 1993: 22–29.

Coppock, Donald R. (INS Deputy Associate Commissioner, Domestic Control). "History: Border Patrol" (unpublished manuscript), available in the library of the INS Historian, Washington, D.C., circa 1968.

Cornelius, Wayne A. *Mexican Migration to the United States: Causes, Consequences, and U.S. Responses*. Cambridge, Mass.: Center for International Studies, Massachusetts Institute of Technology, 1978.

———. "Controlling 'Unwanted' Immigration: Lessons from the United States, 1993–2004," *Journal of Ethnic and Migration Studies* 31, no. 4 (July 2005): 775–794.

———. "Impacts of Border Enforcement on Unauthorized Mexican Migration to the United States." *Border Battles: The U.S. Immigration Debates* (Social Science Research Council, September 26, 2006), http://borderbattles.ssrc.org/ Cornelius/index.html.

———. "Introduction: Does Border Enforcement Deter Unauthorized Immigration?" In *Impacts of Border Enforcement on Mexican Migration: The View from Sending Communities*, edited by Wayne A. Cornelius and Jessa M. Lewis, 1–15. La Jolla, Calif.: Center for Comparative Immigration Studies, University of California, San Diego, 2007.

Cross, Harry E., and James A. Sandos. *Across the Border: Rural Development in Mexico and Recent Migration to the United States*. Berkeley: Institute of Governmental Studies, University of California, Berkeley, 1981.

Curry, Michael. *Work in the World: Geographical Practice and the Written Word.* Minneapolis: University of Minnesota Press, 1996.

Danticat, Edwidge. "Impounded Fathers" (op-ed). *New York Times,* June 17, 2007.

Davis, Kenneth C. "The Founding Immigrants" (op-ed). *New York Times,* July 4, 2007.

Davis, Mike. *City of Quartz: Excavating the Future in Los Angeles.* New York: Verso, 1990.

———. "The Social Origins of the Referendum." *NACLA Report on the Americas* 29, no. 3 (1995): 24–28.

———. *Dead Cities, and Other Tales.* New York: New Press, 2002.

"Death in the Desert" (editorial). *San Diego Union-Tribune,* August 17, 1998.

DeBuys, William. "The Theory and Practice of Borders." *DoubleTake* (Spring 1996): 106–18.

De Genova, Nicholas. *Working the Boundaries: Race, Space, and "Illegality" in Mexican Chicago.* Durham, North Carolina: Duke University Press, 2005.

Delgado, Grace Peña. "At Exclusion's Southern Gate: Changing Categories of Race and Class among Chinese *Fronterizos,* 1882–1904." In *Continental Crossroads: Remapping U.S.-Mexico Borderlands History,* edited by Samuel Truett and Elliot Young, 183–208. Durham, North Carolina: Duke University Press, 2004.

Delgado Wise, Raúl, and Miguel Moctezuma Longoria. "Metamorfosis migratoria y evolución de la estructura productive de Zacatecas (1893–1950)." In *Zacatecas: La Sociedad y Sus Dilemas* (Tomo II), edited by Victor del Real, 69–84. Zacatecas: Maestria en Ciencia Politica, Facultad de Derecho, Universidad Autónoma de Zacatecas, 1993.

Delgado Wise, Raúl, Humberto Márquez Covarrubias, and Héctor Rodríguez Ramírez. "Organizaciones transnacionales de migrantes de desarollo regional en Zacatecas." *Migraciones Internacionales* 2, no. 4 (July–December 2004): 159–181.

Deverell, William. *Whitewashed Adobe: The Rise of Los Angeles and the Remaking of Its Mexican Past.* Berkeley: University of California Press, 2004.

DeWitt, Howard. *Violence in the Fields: California Filipino Farm Labor during the Great Depression.* Saratoga, Calif.: Century Twenty One Publishing, 1980.

Diamond, Sara. "Right-Wing Politics and the Anti-Immigration Cause." *Social Justice* 23, no. 3 (Fall 1996): 154-168.

Dinwoodie, D.H. "Deportation: The Immigration Service and the Chicano Labor Movement in 1930s." *New Mexico Historical Review* 52, no. 3 (1977): 193–206.

Doty, Roxanne Lynn. "Fronteras Compasivas and the Ethics of Unconditional Hospitality." *Millennium: Journal of International Studies,* 35, no. 1 (December 2006): 53–74.

Doty, Roxanne Lynn. "Crossroads of Death." In *The Logics of Biopower and the War on Terror: Living, Dying, Surviving*, edited by Elizabeth Dauphine and Cristina Masters, 3–24. New York: Palgrave MacMillan, 2007.

Dow, Mark. *American Gulag: Inside U.S. Immigration Prisons*. Berkeley: University of California Press, 2004.

Dowty, Alan, *Closed Borders: The Contemporary Assault on Freedom of Movement*. New Haven and London: Yale University Press, 1987.

Doyle, William. "Coastal Commission Rejects Extension of Border Triple Fence: Congressman Calls for Federal Override." *Reflections Quarterly Newsletter* 35, no. 2 (April 2004); available online at http://www.sohosandiego.org/reflections/2004-2/fence.htm.

Drinnon, Richard. *Facing West: The Metaphysics of Indian-Hating and Empire-Building*. Norman, Okla.: University of Oklahoma Press, 1997.

Duncan, Robert H. "The Chinese and the Economic Development of Northern Baja California, 1889–1929." *Hispanic American Historical Review* 74, no. 4 (1994): 615–647.

Dunn, Timothy J. *The Militarization of the U.S.-Mexico Border, 1978–1992: Low-Intensity Conflict Doctrine Comes Home*. Austin: Center for Mexican American Studies, University of Texas at Austin Press, 1996.

Eckels, Richard P. "Hungry Workers, Ripe Crops, and the Non-Existent Mexican Border," *Reporter* 10, no. 8 (April 13, 1954): 28–32.

Ellingwood, Ken. "7 Found Dead in Desert Migrant Corridor." *Los Angeles Times*, August 14, 1998a.

———. "$5,000 Offered in Desert Exposure Deaths." *Los Angeles Times*, August 15, 1998b.

———. *Hard Line: Life and Death on the U.S.-Mexico Border*. New York: Pantheon Books, 2004.

Esbach, Karl, Jacqueline Hagan, and Nestor Rodriguez. "Causes and Trends in Migrant Deaths along the U.S.-Mexico Border, 1985–1998." Houston: Center for Immigration Research, University of Houston, 2001.

———. "Deaths During Undocumented Migration: Trends and Policy Implications in the New Era of Homeland Security." *In Defense of the Alien* 26 (2003): 37–52, http://www.uh.edu/cir/Deaths_during_migration.pdf.

Escobar, Edward J. *Race, Police, and the Making of a Political Identity: Mexican Americans and the Los Angeles Police Department, 1900–1945*. Berkeley: University of California Press, 1999.

Esparza, Salvador. Interview by author. Juchipila, Zacatecas, Mexico. June 2004.

Evans, Christine. "Train Jumping: A Desperate Journey." *Palm Beach Post*, November 11, 2006.

Fairchild, Amy L. *Science at the Borders: Immigrant Medical Inspection and the Shaping of the Modern Industrial Labor Force*. Baltimore: Johns Hopkins University Press, 2003.

Fausset, Richard. "After Police Incident, Some Fear Inglewood Will Take a Beating." *Los Angeles Times*, July 23, 2002.

Feagin, Joe R. "Old Poison in New Bottles: The Deep Roots of Modern Nativism." In *Immigrants Out! The New Nativism and the Anti-Immigrant Impulse in the United States*, edited by Juan F. Perea, 13–43. New York and London: New York University Press, 1997.

Ferguson, Edwin E. "The California Alien Land Law and the Fourteenth Amendment." *California Law Review* 35, no. 1 (March 1947): 61–90.

Fernandes, Deepa. *Targeted: National Security and the Business of Immigration*. New York: Seven Stories Press, 2006.

Fernandez, Celestino, and Lawrence R. Pedroza. "The Border Patrol and News Media Coverage of Undocumented Mexican Immigration during the 1970s: A Quantitative Content Analysis in the Sociology of Knowledge." *California Sociologist* 5, no. 2 (Summer 1982): 1–26.

Fineman, Mark. "Dominican Bones Line Pathway to States." *Los Angeles Times*, May 12, 1998.

Fix, Michael E., and Wendy Zimmerman. "All Under One Roof: Mixed Status Families in an Era of Reform" (research report). Washington, D.C.: Urban Institute, October 6, 1999, http://www.urban.org.

Flamming, Douglas. *Bound for Freedom: Black Los Angeles in Jim Crow America*. Berkeley: University of California Press, 2005.

Fleming, Maria. "A Garden of Honor." *Teaching Tolerance*, no. 13 (Spring 1998); available online at http://www.tolerance.org/teach/magazine/.

Flynn, Michael. "Dondé está la frontera?" *Bulletin of the Atomic Scientists* 58, no. 4, (July/August 2002): 24–35.

Forbes, Jack D. *Warriors of the Colorado: The Yumas of the Quechan Nation and Their Neighbors*. Norman, Okla.: University of Oklahoma Press, 1965.

Fuentes, Jezmin, Henry L'Esperance, Raúl Pérez, and Caitlin White. "Impacts of U.S. Immigration Policies on Migration Behavior." In *Impacts of Border Enforcement on Mexican Migration: The View from Sending Communities*, edited by Wayne A. Cornelius and Jessa M. Lewis, 53–73. La Jolla, California: Center for Comparative Immigration Studies, University of California, San Diego, 2007.

Furillo, Andy. "Toiling under Abuse." *Sacramento Bee*, May 30, 2001, http://www.sacbee.com/static/archive/news/projects/workers/20010520_main.html.

Galarza, Ernesto. *Merchants of Labor: The Mexican Bracero Story*. Charlotte and Santa Barbara: McNally & Loftin, 1964.

Gamio, Manuel. *Mexican Immigration to the United States: A Study of Human Migration and Adjustment*. Chicago: University of Chicago Press, 1930.

Gaouette, Nicole, and Miguel Bustillo. "Immigration's Net Binds Children Too." *Los Angeles Times*, February 10, 2007.

García, Juan Ramon. *Operation Wetback: The Mass Deportation of Mexican Undocumented Workers in 1954*. Westport, Conn., and London, England: Greenwood Press, 1980.

Germani, Clara. "Canals Make Imperial Valley Bloom beneath the Sun." *Christian Science Monitor*. July 10, 1991.

Gilly, Adolfo. *The Mexican Revolution*. New York: New Press, 2005.

Gilmore, Ruth W. "Fatal Couplings of Power and Difference: Notes on Racism and Geography." *The Professional Geographer* 54, no. 1 (2002a): 15–24.

———. "Race and Globalization." In *Geographies of Global Change: Remapping the World*, edited by R. J. Johnston, P. J. Taylor, and M. J. Watts, 261–74. Malden, Mass.: Blackwell Publishers, Ltd., 2002b.

González, Gilbert G. "Company Unions, the Mexican Consulate, and the Imperial Valley Agricultural Strikes, 1928–1934." *Western Historical Quarterly* (Spring 1996): 53–73.

———. *Guest Workers or Colonized Labor? Mexican Labor Migration to the United States*. Boulder, Colorado: Paradigm Publishers, 2006.

González, Gilbert G., and Raúl Fernandez, "Empire and the Origins of Twentieth Century Migration from Mexico to the United States." *Pacific Historical Review* 71, no. 1 (February 2002): 19–57.

Goodspeed, Rob. "A Tale of Both Nogaleses." *Michigan Today* 35, no. 2 (Summer 2003), http://www.umich.edu/news/MT/03/Sum03/tale.html.

Gordon, Linda. *The Great Arizona Orphan Abduction*. Cambridge, Mass.: Harvard University Press, 2001.

Grasmuck, Sheri, and Patricia R. Pessar. *Between Two Islands: Dominican International Migration*. Berkeley: University of California Press, 1991.

Grebler, Leo. *Mexican Immigration to the United States: The Record and Its Implications*. Mexican-American Study Project, Advance Report 2, University of California, Los Angeles, 1966.

Gregory, Steven. *The Devil Behind the Mirror: Globalization and Politics in the Dominican Republic*. Berkeley: University of California Press, 2007.

Griswold del Castillo, Richard. *The Los Angeles Barrio, 1850–1890*. Berkeley: University of California Press, 1979.

———. *The Treaty of Guadalupe Hidalgo: A Legacy of Conflict*. Norman, Okla.: University of Oklahoma Press, 1990.

Gross, Gregory. "300 from China Found in Ensenada." *San Diego Union-Tribune*, April 28, 1993.

Guerin-Gonzales, Camille. *Mexican Workers and American Dreams: Immigration, Repatriation, and California Labor, 1900–1939*. New Brunswick, New Jersey: Rutgers University Press, 1994.

Gutiérrez, David G. *Walls and Mirrors: Mexican Americans, Mexican Immigrants, and the Politics of Ethnicity*. Berkeley, Los Angeles, and London: University of California Press, 1995.

Hall, Stuart. "Race, Culture, and Communications: Looking Backward and Forward at Cultural Studies." *Rethinking Marxism* 5, no. 1 (Spring 1992): 10–18.

Hamilton, Cynthia. "Apartheid in an American City: The Case of the Black Community in Los Angeles" (reprint of article published in the *Los Angeles Weekly*), Los Angeles: Labor/Community Strategy Center, 1987.

Hammer, Joshua. "Hostile Refuge," *Mother Jones*, January/February 2006.

Haney López, Ian F. *White by Law: The Legal Construction of Race*. New York and London: New York University Press, 1996.

———. *Racism on Trial: The Chicano Fight for Justice*. Cambridge, Mass.: Harvard University Press, 2003.

"Hard Line on Human Coyotes" (editorial). *Los Angeles Times*, August 20, 1998.

Harris, Elizabeth. *The Valley Imperial* (Books I and II). Holtville, Calif.: Imperial Valley Pioneers, 1956–1958 (revised and reprinted by the Imperial County Historical Society in 1991).

Harris, Nigel, *Thinking the Unthinkable: The Immigration Myth Exposed*. London and New York: I. B. Tauris Publishers, 2002.

Harris, Olivia. "The Deadliest Voyage." *First Post*, September 15, 2006, http://www.thefirstpost.co.uk/index.php?menuID=2&subID=674.

Heizer, Robert F., and Alan J. Almquist. *The Other Californians: Prejudice and Discrimination under Spain, Mexico, and the United States to 1920*. Berkeley: University of California Press, 1971.

Hendricks, William O. "Developing San Diego's Desert Empire." *Journal of San Diego History* 17, no. 3 (Summer 1971), http://www.sandiegohistory.org/journal/71summer/desert.htm.

Henry, Mark. "Images Are All that Are Left of Quest for a Better Life." *Press Enterprise* (Riverside, Calif.), August 21, 1998.

Hernandez Jauregui, Hugo Horacio. Interview by author. Bancomer, Juchipla branch, Juchipila, Zacatecas, Mexico. June 2004.

Herzog, Lawrence A. *Where North Meets South: Cities, Space, and Politics on the U.S.-Mexico Border*. Austin: Center for Mexican American Studies, University of Texas at Austin, 1990.

Heyman, Josiah McC. "United States Surveillance over Mexican Lives at the Border: Snapshots of an Emerging Regime." *Human Organization* 58, no. 4 (1999a): 429–37.

———. "Why Interdiction? Immigration Control at the United States–Mexico Border." *Regional Studies* 33, no. 7 (1999b): 619–30.

Hing, Bill Ong. *Deporting Our Souls: Values, Morality, and Immigration Policy*. Cambridge, U.K.: Cambridge University Press, 2006.

Holmes, Steven A., and Steven Greenhouse. "Bush Choice for Labor Post Withdraws and Cites Furor of Illegal Immigrant Issue." *New York Times*, January 10, 2001.

Horsman, Reginald. *Race and Manifest Destiny: The Origins of American Racial Anglo-Saxonism*. Cambridge, Mass.: Harvard University Press, 1981.

Huffaker, Sandy. "Border Fight Focuses on Water, Not Immigration." *New York Times*, July 7, 2006.

Hundley, Norris. *Water and the West: The Colorado River Compact and the Politics of Water in the American West*. Berkeley: University of California Press, 1975.

———. *The Great Thirst: Californians and Water: A History*, rev. ed. Berkeley: University of California Press, 2001.

Ichioka, Yuji. *The Issei: The World of the First Generation Japanese Immigrants, 1885–1924*. New York: Free Press, 1988.

Iwata, Masakazu. *Planted in Good Soil: The History of the Issei in United States Agriculture*, 2 vols. New York: Peter Lang, 1992.

Jacobs, Paul. "Wilson Often Battled INS, Letters Show." *Los Angeles Times*, September 25, 1995.

Japanese American National Museum. *Los Angeles's Boyle Heights*. Charleston, S.C.: Arcadia Publishing, 2005.

Johnson, Benjamin Heber. *Revolution in Texas: How a Forgotten Rebellion and Its Bloody Suppression Turned Mexicans into Americans*. New Haven: Yale University Press, 2003.

Johnson, Kevin R. "Open Borders?" *UCLA Law Review* 51, no. 1 (October 2003): 193–265.

———. *The "Huddled Masses" Myth: Immigration and Civil Rights*. Philadelphia: Temple University Press, 2004.

Jones, Richard C. *Ambivalent Journey: U.S. Migration and Economic Mobility in North-Central Mexico*. Tucson: University of Arizona Press, 1995.

Kanstroom, Daniel. *Deportation Nation: Outsiders in American History*. Cambridge, Mass.: Harvard University Press, 2007.

Kateel, Subhash, and Aarti Shahani. "From the Ground Up: Families Organizing Against Deportation, For Freedom." In *Keeping Out the Other: A Critical Introduction to Immigration Enforcement Today*, edited by David Brotherton and Philip Kretsedemas. New York: Columbia University Press, forthcoming 2008.

Keim, Samuel M., Mary Z. Mays, Bruce Parks, Erik Pytlak, Robin M. Harris, and Michael A. Kent, "Estimating the Incidence of Heat-Related Deaths Among Immigrants in Pima County, Arizona." *Journal of Immigrant and Minority Health* 8, no. 2 (April 2006): 185–91.

Kelley, Robin D. G. "The Riddle of the Zoot: Malcolm Little and Black Cultural Politics during World War II." In *Race and the Subject of Masculinities*, edited by Harry Stecopoulos and Michael Uebel, 231–252. Durham, North Carolina: Duke University Press, 1997.

Kelly, David. "Salton Sea Is At a Crucial Juncture." *Los Angeles Times*, April 30, 2007.

King, Patricia and Donna Foote. "Across the Borderline." *Newsweek*, May 31, 1993: 25.

Krauthammer, Charles. "Good Fences" (op-ed). *Washington Post*, June 15, 2007.

Kwong, Peter. *Forbidden Workers: Illegal Chinese Immigrants and American Labor*. New York: New Press, 1997.

Laflin, P. "The Salton Sea: California's Overlooked Treasure." *Periscope*, Coachella Valley Historical Society, Indio, California, 1995, http://www.sci.sdsu.edu/salton/ Periscope-SaltonSea.html.

Landis, Christopher. *In Search of El Dorado: The Salton Sea*. Palm Springs, Calif.: Palm Springs Desert Museum, 2000.

Lau, Angela. "Boatload of Chinese Seized Here." *San Diego Union-Tribune*, May 13, 1993.

Laufer, Peter. *Wetback Nation: The Case for Opening the Mexican-American Border*. Chicago: Ivan R. Dee, 2004.

LeDuff, Charles. "Just This Side of the Treacherous Border, Here Lies John Doe." *New York Times*, September 24, 2004.

Lee, Erika. *At America's Gate: Chinese Immigration during the Exclusion Era, 1882–1943*. Chapel Hill: University of North Carolina Press, 2003.

Leiken, Robert S. and Steven Brooke. "The Quantitative Analysis of Terrorism and Immigration: An Initial Exploration." *Terrorism and Political Violence* 18 (2006): 503–521.

Leonard, Karen Isaksen. *Making Ethnic Choices: California's Punjabi Mexican Americans*. Philadelphia: Temple University Press, 1992.

Levitt, Peggy. *The Transnational Villagers*. Berkeley: University of California Press, 2001.

Lewis, Sasha G. *Slave Trade Today: American Exploitation of Illegal Aliens*. Boston: Beacon Press, 1979.

Limerick, Patricia Nelson. *Desert Passages: Encounters with the American Deserts*. Boulder, Colorado: University of Colorado Press, 1989.

Lindstrom, David P. *The Relationship Between Temporary United States Migration and Fertility in a Rural Mexican Township*. PhD diss., Department of Sociology, University of Chicago, 1995, photocopied and printed by UNI Dissertation Services, Ann Arbor, Mich.

Livernois, Joe. *Hetzel the Photographer: Impressions of Imperial Valley*. Fresno, Calif.: Pioneer Publishing, 1982.

Loewen, James W. *Sundown Towns: A Hidden Dimension of American Racism*. New York: New Press, 2005.

Logan, John, Deidre Oakley, Polly Smith, Jacob Stowell, and Brian Stults. "Separating the Children" (report), Albany: Lewis Mumford Center, State University of New York at Albany, December 28, 2001, http://mumford1.dyndns.org/cen2000/ index.html.

Logan, Michael H. "Immigration and Relative Deprivation: The Tijuana-San Ysidro Border Station." Master's thesis, Department of Anthropology, San Diego State College, 1969.

London, Joan, and Henry Anderson. *So Shall Ye Reap*. New York: Thomas Y. Crowell, 1970.

"Looking for Answers" (editorial). *Imperial Valley Press*, August 20, 1998.

López Robles, Raúl. *Monografia de Juchipila*, self-published in Mexico, 2000 (2nd ed.).

———. Interview by author. Juchipila, Zacatecas, Mexico. June 2004.

Lucero, Héctor Manuel. "Peopling Baja California." In *Postborder City: Cultural Spaces of Bajalta California*, edited by Michael Dear and Gustavo Leclerc, 83–115. New York: Routledge, 2003.

Luibheid, Eithne. *Entry Denied: Controlling Sexuality at the Border*. Minneapolis: University of Minnesota Press, 2002.

Marcelli, Enrico. "Undocumented Latino Immigrant Workers: The Los Angeles Experience." In *Illegal Immigration in America: A Reference Handbook*, edited by David W. Haines and Karen E. Rosenblum, 193-231. Westport, Conn.: Greenwood Press, 1999.

Maril, Robert Lee. *Patrolling Chaos: The U.S. Border Patrol in Deep South Texas*. Lubbock, Tex.: Texas Tech University Press, 2004.

Marosi, Richard. "Families Reach Out Across Border." *Los Angeles Times*, May 10, 2004a.

———. "Border Jumpers Leave Their Imprint on a Besieged Town." *Los Angeles Times*, June 3, 2004b.

———. "Border Crossing Deaths Set a 12-Month Record." *Los Angeles Times*, October 1, 2005.

———. "Feel the Rush of a Smuggler." *Los Angeles Times*, January 25, 2006.

———. "New Tactics Disrupt Illegal Immigration." *Los Angeles Times*, March 21, 2007.

Martinez, Andrés. "Policing a Fine, Porous Line across the Perilous West Desert Corridor." *New York Times*, October 14, 2002.

Martínez, Oscar J. *Troublesome Border*. Tucson: University of Arizona Press, 1995.

——— (ed.). *U.S.-Mexico Borderlands: Historical and Contemporary Perspectives*. Wilmington, Del.: Scholarly Resources, 1996.

Martínez Zepada, Jorge, José A. Estrada Lázaro, and Martha Dominguez Medina. "Del trazado de la linea internacional a la colonización bajo Delta del Colorado." In *Mexicali: Una historia*, edited by Jorge Martínez Zepada and Lourdes Romero Navarrete, 89–146. Mexicali, Baja California, Mexico: Instituto de Investigaciones Históricas, Universidad Autonoma de Baja California, 1991.

Massey, Doreen. "Power-geometry and a Progressive Sense of Place." In *Mapping the Futures: Local Cultures, Global Change*, edited by John Bird, Barry Curtis, Tim Putnam, and Lisa Tickner, 59–69. London: Routledge, 1993.

———. *For Space*. London and Thousand Oaks, Calif.: Sage Publications, 2005.

Massey, Douglas S., and Nancy A. Denton. *American Apartheid: Segregation and the Making of the Underclass*. Cambridge, Mass.: Harvard University Press, 1994.

Massey, Douglas S., Jorge Durand, and Nolan J. Malone. *Beyond Smoke and Mirrors: Mexican Immigration in an Era of Economic Integration*. New York: Russell Sage Foundation, 2002.

Mattingly, Doreen J. "Where are the Women?" *Antipode* 36, no. 1 (2004): 142–45.

Mayer, Arno. *The Furies: Violence and Terror in the French and Russian Revolutions*. Princeton, New Jersey: Princeton University Press, 2002.

McAllen, Lowry. "Echoes of a Village Exodus." *Américas* 51, no. 6 (Nov. 1999): 40–45.

McConahay, Mary Jo. "They Die in Brooks County." *Texas Observer*, June 1, 2007; available online at http://www.texasobserver.org/article.php?aid=2509.

McDonald, William F. "Illegal Immigration: Crime, Ramifications, and Control (The American Experience)." In *Crime and Law Enforcement in the Global Village*, edited by William McDonald, 65–86. Cincinnati: Anderson Publishing, 1997.

McKinley, James C., Jr. "Tougher Tactics Deter Migrants at U.S. Border." *New York Times*, February 21, 2007.

McWilliams, Carey. *Factories in the Field: The Story of Migratory Farm Labor in California*. Boston: Little, Brown, 1939.

———. *California: The Great Exception*. Westport, Conn.: Greenwood Press, 1949.

———. *North from Mexico: The Spanish-Speaking People of the United States*. New York: Greenwood Press, 1968 (originally published in 1949).

Menchaca, Martha. *The Mexican Outsiders: A Community History of Marginalization and Discrimination in California*. Austin, Tex.: University of Texas Press, 1995.

Meeropol, Rachel. "The Post-9/11 Terrorism Investigation and Immigration Detention." In *America's Disappeared: Secret Imprisonment, Detainees, and the "War on Terror,"* edited by Rachel Meeropol, 144–170. New York: Seven Stories Press, 2005.

Meldrum, Andrew. "60 Migrants Feared Drowned Fleeing from Zimbabwe." *Guardian*, January 20, 2006.

Miller, David and Sohail H. Hashmi. *Boundaries and Justice: Diverse Ethical Perspectives*. Princeton, N.J.: Princeton University Press, 2001.

Miller, Jim. "Just Another Day in Paradise? An Episodic History of Rebellion and Repression in America's Finest City." In *Under the Perfect Sun: The San Diego Tourists Never See*, edited by in Mike Davis, Kelly Mayhew, and Jim Miller, 159–261. New York: New Press, 2005.

Milton, Pat. "Trade Center Plotters May Have Left U.S." *San Diego Union-Tribune*, March 6, 1993.

Mitchell, Don. *The Lie of the Land: Migrant Workers and the California Landscape*. Minneapolis: University of Minnesota Press, 1996.

Molina, Natalia. *Fit to Be Citizens: Public Health and Race in Los Angeles, 1879–1939*. Berkeley: University of California Press, 2006.

Monroy, Douglas. *Rebirth: Mexican Los Angeles from the Great Migration to the Great Depression*. Berkeley: University of California Press, 1999.

Montes, Eduardo. "Migrant Deaths Down along Border." ABC News, October 3, 2006, http://abcnews.go.com/US/wireStory?id=2524719.

Morganthau, Tom. "America: Still a Melting Pot?" *Newsweek*, August 9, 1993: 16–23.

Mozingo, Joe. "A Tragic Journey Home." *Los Angeles Times*, August 21, 1998.

Mueller , John. "Is There Still a Terrorist Threat?" *Foreign Affairs* (September/October 2006), http://www.foreignaffairs.org/20060901facomment85501/john-mueller/ is-there-still-a-terrorist-threat.html.

Murr, Andrew. "A Nasty Turn on Immigrants." *Newsweek*, August 23, 1993: 28.

Nadelmann, Ethan A. *Cops across Borders: The Internationalization of U.S. Criminal Law Enforcement*. University Park, Penn.: Pennsylvania State University Press, 1993.

Nevins, Joseph. *Operation Gatekeeper: The Rise of the "Illegal Alien" and the Making of the U.S.-Mexico Boundary*, New York: Routledge, 2002.

———. "Thinking Out of Bounds: A Critical Analysis of Academic and Human Rights Writings on Migrant Deaths in the U.S.-Mexico Border Region." *Migraciones Internacionales* 2, no. 2 (July–December 2003): 171–190.

———. "From a Boundary of Death to One of Life." *Counterpunch*, November 1, 2005a, http://www.counterpunch.org/nevins11012005.html.

———. "A Beating Worse than Death: Imagining and Contesting Violence in the U.S.-Mexico Borderlands." *AmeriQuests* 2, no. 1 (2005b), http://ejournals.library.vanderbilt.edu/ameriquests/viewarticle.php?id=73.

———. "Dying for a Cup of Coffee? Migrant Deaths in the US-Mexico Border Region in a Neoliberal Age." *Geopolitics* 12, no. 2 (2007): 228–247.

Ngai, Mae M. *Impossible Subjects: Illegal Aliens and the Making of Modern America*. Princeton, N.J.: Princeton University Press, 2004.

Nguyen, Tram. *We Are All Suspects Now: Untold Stories from Immigrant Communities after 9/11*. Boston: Beacon Press, 2005.

Normark, Don. *Chávez Ravine, 1949: A Los Angeles Story*. San Francisco: Chronicle Books, 1999.

Norris, Robert M., and Robert W. Webb. *Geology of California*. New York: John Wiley and Sons, 1976.

Notimex. "Viven en Mexico la mitad de los trabajadores del condado Imperial." *Imagen* (Zacatecas), August 24, 1998.

Obsatz, Sharyn. "Dangers: Increased U.S. Border Security is Forcing Migrants to Attempt Risky Routes into the Country." *Press-Enterprise* (Riverside, Calif.), March 30, 2003.

Odens, Peter. *The Desert Trackers (Men of the Border Patrol)*. Yuma: Self-published, 1981 (second printing, originally published 1975).

Office of Public Affairs, Immigration and Naturalization Service (Laguna Niguel, California), U.S. Department of Justice. "$5,000 Reward Offered for Alien Smuggler Information" (press release), August 14, 1998.

Orenstein, Dara. "Void for Vagueness: Mexicans and the Collapse of Miscegenation Law in California." *Pacific Historical* Review 74, no. 3 (August 2005): 367–407.

Ostrow, Ronald J. "Saxbe Calls Illegal Aliens a U.S. Crisis." *Los Angeles Times*, October 31, 1974.

Padilla, Juan Manuel. "Emigración internacional y remesas en Zacatecas." *Comercio Exterior* (Banco Nacional de Comercio Exterior, Mexico City) 50, no. 5 (May 2000): 363–370.

Palafox, José, and Matthew Jardine, "Hardening the Line: The Growing American War on 'Illegals,'" *Colorlines*, no. 3 (Winter 1999): 20–22.

Pardo, Mary S. *Mexican American Women Activists: Identity and Resistance in Two Los Angeles Communities*. Philadelphia: Temple University Press, 1998.

Pascoe, Peggy. "Race, Gender, and Intercultural Relations: The Case of Interracial Marriage." *Frontiers: A Journal of Women Studies* 12, no. 1. (1991): 5–18.

———. "Miscegenation Law, Court Cases, and Ideologies of 'Race' in Twentieth-Century America." *Journal of American History* 83, no. 1 (June 1996): 44–69.

Pawel, Miriam. "Decisions of Long Ago Shape the Union Today." *Los Angeles Times*, January 10, 2006.

Perea, Juan F. (ed.) *Immigrants Out! The New Nativism and the Anti-Immigrant Impulse in the United States*. New York and London: New York University Press, 1997.

———. "A Brief History of Race and the U.S.-Mexican Border: Tracing the Trajectories of Conquest." *UCLA Law Review*. 51, no. 1 (October 2003): 283–312.

Perkins, Clifford Alan. *Border Patrol: With the U.S. Immigration Service on the Mexican Boundary 1910–1954*. University of Texas at El Paso: Texas Western Press, 1978.

Perry, Tony. "Clash Brews Over Tainted Waters." *Los Angeles Times*, February 24, 2006.

Petras, Elizabeth. "The Role of National Boundaries in a Cross-National Labour Market." *International Journal of Urban and Regional Research* 4, no. 2 (June 1980): 157–195.

Pitt, Leonard. *The Decline of the Californios: A Social History of the Spanish-Speaking Californians, 1846–1890*. Berkeley and Los Angeles: University of California Press, 1998 (originally published in 1966).

Polaski, Sandra. "Jobs, Wages, and Household Income." In *NAFTA's Promise and Reality: Lessons from Mexico for the Hemisphere*, edited by John J. Audley et al., 11–37. Washington, D.C.:

Carnegie Endowment for International Peace, November 2003; available online at http://www.carnegieendowment.org/files/nafta1.pdf.

Politzer, Maria. "'It's Our Job to Stop That Dream': The Endless, Futile Work of the Border Patrol." *Reason*, April 2007; available online at http://www.reason.com/news/show/119089.html.

Poole, Jean Bruce, and Tevvy Ball. *El Pueblo: The Historic Heart of Los Angeles*. Los Angeles: Getty Conservation Institute and J. Paul Getty Museum, 2002.

Popkin, James and Dorian Friedman. "Return to Sender—Please." *U.S. News & World Report*, June 21, 1993: 32.

Price, Patricia L. *Dry Place: Landscapes of Belonging and Exclusion*. Minneapolis: University of Minnesota Press, 2004.

Pulido, Laura. *Black, Brown, Yellow, and Left: Radical Activism in Los Angeles*. Berkeley: University of California Press, 2006.

Rappleye, Charles. "Mexico, America, and the Continental Divide." *Virginia Quarterly Review* 83, no. 2 (Spring 2007): 61–82.

Reeves, Richard. "Boyle Heights and Beyond." *New Yorker*, September 14, 1981: 116+.

Reisler, Mark. *By the Sweat of their Brow: Mexican Immigrant Labor in the United States, 1900–1940*. Westport, Conn., and London: Greenwood Press, 1976.

Reisner, Marc. *Cadillac Desert: The American West and Its Disappearing Water*. New York: Penguin, 1993.

Reséndez, Andrés. *Changing National Identities at the Frontier: Texas and New Mexico 1800–1850*. Cambridge, U.K.: Cambridge University Press, 2006.

Reuters. "Mexico Migrants Use Cycles to Cross Arizona Desert." August 21, 2006a.

———. "One in Six Migrants Dies Trying to Reach Canaries." December 27, 2006b.

Riccardi, Nicholas. "Some Border Patrol Agents Take a Chance on Love." *Los Angeles Times*, December 26, 2005.

Richmond, Anthony. *Global Apartheid: Refugees, Racism, and the New World Order*. Toronto: Oxford University Press, 1994.

Rico, Carlos. "Migration and U.S.-Mexican Relations, 1966–1986." In *Western Hemisphere Immigration and United States Foreign Policy*, edited by Christopher Mitchell, 221–283. University Park, Penn.: Pennsylvania State University Press, 1992.

Riley, Michael. "Moving Targets: Part 4." *Denver Post*, March 7, 2007.

Robinovitz, Karen. "In Pursuit of Fabulousness." *New York Times*, August 13, 2004.

Romero, Simon. "Lights out in the Dominican Republic." *New York Times*, August 14, 2004a.

———. "Nightmare at Sea Shatters Dreams in a Dominican Town." *New York Times*, August 16, 2004b.

———. "Dominican Resumes Presidency on Stern Note." *New York Times*, August 17, 2004c.

Romo, David Dorado. *Ringside Seat to a Revolution: An Underground Cultural History of El Paso and Juárez, 1893–1923*. El Paso, Tex.: Cinco Puntos Press, 2005.

Romo, Ricardo. *East Los Angeles: History of a Barrio*. Austin: University of Texas Press, 1983.

Root, Jay. "Aiding Homeland is Goal of Many." *Deseret News* (Salt Lake City), March 26, 2006.

Rorty, James. "Lettuce—with American Dressing." *Nation* 140, no. 3545 (May 15, 1935): 575–576.

Rosas, Gilberto. "The Fragile Ends of War: Forging the United States-Mexico Border and Borderlands Consciousness," *Social Text* 25, no. 2 (Summer 2007): 81–102.

Ross, John. *The Annexation of Mexico: From the Aztecs to the I.M.F.* Monroe, Maine: Common Courage Press, 1998.

Rotella, Sebastian. *Twilight on the Line: Underworlds and Politics at the U.S.-Mexico Border*. New York and London: W. W. Norton, 1998.

Rowling, Nick. *Commodities: How the World Was Taken to Market*. London: Free Association Books, 1987.

Rubio-Goldsmith, Raquel, M. Melissa McCormick, Daniel Martinez, and Inez Magdalena Duarte. *The "Funnel Effect" and Recovered Bodies of Unauthorized Migrants Processed by the Pima County Office of the Medical Examiner, 1990–2005*. Report submitted to the Pima County Board of Supervisors, Tucson: Binational Migration Institute, University of Arizona (October 2006); available online at http://www.ailf.org/ipc/policybrief/policybrief_020607.pdf.

Ruiz, Ramón Eduardo. *On the Rim of Mexico: Encounters of the Rich and Poor*. Boulder, Colorado: Westview Press, 2000.

Rumbaut, Rubén G., and Walter A. Ewing. "The Myth of Immigrant Criminality and the Paradox of Assimilation: Incarceration Rates among Native and Foreign-Born Men" (Special Report). Washington, D.C.: Immigration Policy Center, American Immigration Law Foundation, Spring 2007; available online at http://www.ailf.org.

Sampson, Robert J., Jeffrey D. Morenoff, and Stephen Raudenbush. "Social Anatomy of Racial and Ethnic Disparities in Violence." *American Journal of Public Health* 95, no. 2 (February 2005): 224–232.

Sánchez, George J. *Becoming Mexican American: Ethnicity, Culture, and Identity in Chicano Los Angeles, 1900–1945*. New York and Oxford: Oxford University Press, 1993.

———. "Working at the Crossroads: American Studies for the 21st Century" (Presidential Address to the American Studies Association, November 9, 2001). *American Quarterly* 54, no. 1 (March 2002): 1–23.

———. "'What's Good for Boyle Heights is Good for the Jews': Creating Multiracialism on the Eastside During the 1950s." *American Quarterly* 56, no. 3 (2004): 633–661.

Sandos, James A. *Rebellion in the Borderlands: Anarchism and the Plan of San Diego, 1904–1923*. Norman, Okla.: University of Oklahoma Press, 1992.

Sapkota, Sanjeeb, Harold W. Kohl III, Julie Gilchrist, Jay McAuliffe, Bruce Parks, Bob England, Tim Flood, Mack Sewell, Dennis Perrotta, Miguel Escobedo, Corrine E. Stern, David Zane, and Kurt B. Nolte. "Unauthorized Border Crossings and Migrant Deaths: Arizona, New Mexico, and El Paso, Texas, 2002–2003." *American Journal of Public Health* 96, no. 7 (July 2006): 1282–1287.

Schantz, Eric Michael. "All Night at the Owl: The Social and Political Relations of Mexicali's Red-Light District, 1913–1925." *Journal of the Southwest* 43, no. 4 (Winter 2001): 549–602.

Schrag, Peter. *Paradise Lost: California's Experience, America's Future*. New York: New Press, 1998.

Scully, Megan. "Lawmaker Renews Call to Build Fence Guarding Border." *GOVEXEC.com*, May 24, 2006; available online at http://www.govexec.com/dailyfed/0506/052406cdpm2.htm.

Shadow of Hope (television documentary), directed by Ken Verdoia and Nancy Green. Salt Lake City, Utah: KUED Productions, 2004, transcript available online at http://www.kued.org/productions/shadowofhope/index.php.

Sharma, Nandita. *Home Economics: Nationalism and the Making of "Migrant Workers" in Canada*. Toronto: University of Toronto Press, 2006.

Sides, Josh. *L.A. City Limits: African American Los Angeles from the Great Depression to the Present*. Berkeley: University of California Press, 2003.

Silko, Leslie Marmon. "The Border Patrol State." In *Puro Border: Dispatches, Snapshots & Grafitti from La Frontera*, edited by Luis Humberto Croswaithe, John William Byrd, and Bobby Bird, 72–78. El Paso, Tex.: Cinco Puntos Press, 2003.

Sparke, Matthew B. "A Neoliberal Nexus: Economy, Security and the Biopolitics of Citizenship on the Border." *Political Geography* 25, no. 2 (February 2006): 151–180.

Spike, Paul. "How America Inspired the Third Reich." *First Post*, May 31, 2007, http://www.thefirstpost.co.uk/index.php?storyID=7083.

Stannard, David E. *American Holocaust: The Conquest of the New World*. New York: Oxford University Press, 1992.

Steinbeck, John. *The Harvest Gypsies: On the Road to the Grapes of Wrath*. Berkeley: Heyday Books, 1988.

Stephanson, Anders. *Manifest Destiny: American Expansionism and the Empire of Right*. New York: Hill and Wang, 1995.

Stern, Alexandra Minna. *Eugenic Nation: Faults and Frontiers of Better Breeding in Modern America*. Berkeley: University of California Press, 2005.

Stern, Marcus. "Back in '89, Pete Wilson Wasn't So Adamant About Migrant Issue." *San Diego Union-Tribune*, September 4, 1993.

———. "In '83, Wilson Helped Curb INS Searches." *San Diego Union-Tribune*, September 17, 1994.

Street, Richard Steven. "The Lettuce Strike Story." *Nation* 230, no. 2, January 19, 1980.

———. *Beasts of the Field: A Narrative History of California Farmworkers, 1769–1913*. Stanford, Calif.: Stanford University Press, 2004a.

———. *Photographing Farmworkers in California*. Stanford, Calif.: Stanford University Press, 2004b.

Streitfeld, David. "Salton City: A Land of Dreams and Dead Fish." *Los Angeles Times*, July 1, 2007.

Takaki, Ronald. *A Different Mirror: A History of Multicultural America*. Boston and New York: Little, Brown, 1993.

Taylor H., and Lawrence Douglas. "El contrabando de chinos a lo largo de la frontera entre México y Estados Unidos, 1882–1931." *Frontera Norte* 6, no. 11 (January–June 1994): 41–57.

Taylor, Paul S. *Mexican Labor in the United States Imperial Valley*. University of California Publications in Economics 6, no. 1 (1928): 1–94. Berkeley: University of California Press.

Thomas, Rich. "The Economic Cost of Immigration." *Newsweek*, August 9, 1993: 18–19.

Thompson, Ginger. "An Exodus of Migrant Families Is Bleeding Mexico's Heartland." *New York Times*, June 17, 2001: 11.

———. "Mexico Worries About Its Own Southern Border." *New York Times*, June 18, 2006.

Torpey, John. *The Invention of the Passport: Surveillance, Citizenship and the State*. Cambridge, U.K.: Cambridge University Press, 2000.

Transactional Records Action Clearinghouse. "Immigration Enforcement: The Rhetoric, the Reality." Report prepared by the Transactional Records Action Clearinghouse, Syracuse University, May 28, 2007, http://trac.syr.edu/immigration/ reports/178.

Truett, Samuel. *Fugitive Landscapes: The Forgotten History of the U.S.-Mexico Borderlands*. New Haven, Conn.: Yale University Press, 2006.

Urrea, Luis Alberto. *The Devil's Highway: A True Story*. New York: Little, Brown, 2004.

U.S. Commission on Civil Rights. "Presentation on Civil and Human Rights Implications of U.S. Southwest Border Policy" (transcript of proceedings). November 14, 2002; available online at http://www.usccr.gov/pubs/migrant/present/trans.htm.

U.S. Congress, Subcommittee on International Law, Immigration, and Refugees of the Committee on the Judiciary, House of Representatives, 103rd Congress. "Immigration-related Issues in the North American Free Trade Agreement" (November 3, 1993) Washington, D.C.: U.S. Government Printing Office, 1994.

U.S. General Accounting Office (U.S. GAO). *Illegal Immigration: Border Crossing Deaths Have Doubled Since 1995; Border Patrol's Efforts to Prevent Deaths Have Not Been Fully Evaluated*, (report number GAO-06-770), Washington, D.C.: U.S. General Accounting Office, August 2006.

U.S. Immigration and Naturalization Service (U.S. INS). *An Immigrant Nation: United States Regulation of Immigration, 1798–1991*. Washington, D.C.: Immigration and Naturalization Service, U.S. Department of Justice, June 18, 1991.

Varsanyi, Monica. "The Rise and Fall (and Rise?) of Non-citizen Voting: Immigration and the Shifting Scales of Citizenship and Suffrage in the United States." *Space and Polity* 9, no. 2 (August 2005): 113–134.

Varzally, Allison. "Romantic Crossings: Making Love, Family, and Non-Whiteness in California, 1925–1950." *Journal of American Ethnic History* 23, no. 1 (Fall 2003): 3–54.

Vázquez, Josefina Zoraida and Lorenzo Meyer. *The United States and Mexico*. Chicago and London: University of Chicago Press, 1985.

Vélez-Ibáñez, Carlos G. *Border Visions: Mexican Cultures of the Southwest United States*. Tucson: University of Arizona Press, 1997.

Vidal, Gore. *Imperial America: Reflections on the United States of Amnesia*. New York: Nation Books, 2004.

Vila, Pablo. *Crossing Borders, Reinforcing Borders: Social Categories, Metaphors and Narrative Identities on the U.S.–Mexico Border*. Austin: University of Texas Press, 2000.

Waddingham, Gladys. *The History of Inglewood*. Inglewood, Calif.: Historical Society of Centinela Valley, 1994.

Walczak, Lee. "Why Clinton Can't Keep His Eyes off California." *Business Week*, June 13, 1994: 51.

Waldinger, Roger. "The Bounded Community: Turning Foreigners into Americans in 21st Century Los Angeles." *Ethnic and Racial Studies* 30, no. 7 (2007): 341–374.

Walker, Richard. "California Rages against the Dying of the Light." *New Left Review*, no. 209 (January/February 1995): 42–74.

———. "California's Collision of Race and Class." *Representations* no. 55 (Summer 1996): 163–183.

———. *The Conquest of Bread: 150 Years of Agribusiness in California*. New York: New Press, 2004.

Walters, Jana. "Illegal Immigration: The Making of Myth." Unpublished paper completed for a graduate seminar in sociology at the University of Texas at Austin. 1990.

Weber, Devra Anne. "The Organizing of Mexicano Agricultural Workers: Imperial Valley, and Los Angeles, 1928–1934, an Oral History Approach." *Aztlán* 3, no. 2 (1972): 307–347.

Weinberg, Albert K. *Manifest Destiny: A Study of Nationalist Expansionism in American History*. Chicago: Quadrangle Books, 1963 (originally published in 1935 by Johns Hopkins University Press).

Weissert, Will. "Vehicle Crossings More Common at Border." Associated Press, June 19, 2006, http://www.newsmax.com/archives/articles/2006/6/19/153313.shtml.

Welch, William M. "In Age of Terror, U.S. Fears Tunnels Pose Bigger Threat." *USA Today*, March 1, 2006.

"Wetbacks Swarm In: Mexicans Disrupt Border Economy by Sneaking over for Low Wages." *Life* 39, no. 21, May 21, 1951: 33–37.

Wild, Mark. "'So Many Children at Once and so Many Kinds': Schools and Ethno-racial Boundaries in Early Twentieth-Century Los Angeles." *Western Historical Quarterly* 33, no. 4 (Winter 2002): 453–478.

Williams, T. Harry. *The History of American Wars: From 1745 to 1918*. New York: Knopf, 1981.

Wilmoth, G. C. "Mexican Border Procedure" (Lecture No. 23, Second Series, November 19, 1934). Washington, D.C.: Immigration and Naturalization Service, U.S. Department of Labor, 1934.

Wise, Amanda. *Exile and Return among the East Timorese*. Philadelphia: University of Pennsylvania Press, 2006.

Wixon, I. F. "Immigration Border Patrol" (Lecture No. 7, March 19, 1934). Washington, D.C.: Immigration and Naturalization Service, U.S. Department of Labor, 1934.

Wolf, Eric. *Europe and the People Without History*. Berkeley: University of California Press, 1980.

Wollenberg, Charles. "'Huelga,' 1928 Style: The Imperial Valley Cantaloupe Workers' Strike." *Pacific Historical Review* 38, no. 1 (February 1969): 45–58.

Worster, Donald. *Rivers of Empire: Water, Aridity, and the Growth of the American West*. New York: Pantheon Books, 1985.

Wright, Angus. *The Death of Ramón González: The Modern Agricultural Dilemma* (revised edition). Austin, Tex.: University of Texas Press: 2005.

Wright, Harold Bell. *The Winning of Barbara Worth*. Gretna, Louisiana: Pelican Publishing, 1999 (originally published in 1911).

Zabin, Carol, and Luis Escala. "From Civic Association to Political Participation: Mexican Hometown Associations and Mexican Immigrant Political Empowerment in Los Angeles." *Frontera Norte* 14, no. 27 (2002).

Zolberg, Aristide. *A Nation By Design: Immigration Policy in the Fashioning of America*. New York: Russell Sage Foundation; Cambridge, Mass.: Harvard University Press, 2006.

Zucker, Norman L., and Naomi Flink Zucker. *Desperate Crossings: Seeking Refuge in America*. Armonk, N.Y., and London: M. E. Sharpe, 1996.

FILES FROM THE NATIONAL ARCHIVES AND RECORDS ADMINISTRATION (NARA) IN WASHINGTON, D.C.

Subject Description of File	*Date*	*File Number*
Enforcement along the Mexican border	February 5, 1918	54261/276
Proposal to establish an immigration patrol service on the land boundaries	April 29, 1918	54261/267
Letter from Austin Spurlock, Inspector-in-Charge, Calexico to INS District Director in Los Angeles	October 24, 1934	4302/44

NOTES

ONE **THE BODIES**

1. See Appendix A for a map of the Imperial Valley and Southern California.
2. Throughout this book, I use the word "boundary" when referring to the actual territorial line between Mexico and the United States. The "border" herein refers to a region, the zone of transition between two countries that share a boundary.
3. For a link to photographs of recovered migrant corpses, see McConahay 2007, online version.
4. Associated Press 1998a.
5. Lee 2003.
6. Bailey et al. 1996; Cornelius 2005; Esbach et al. 2001 and 2003; GAO 2006; Marosi 2005; Montes 2006; see also Annerino 1999.
7. See Cornelius 2005; Esbach et al. 2003; Keim et al. 2006; Rubio-Goldsmith et al. 2007; Sapkota et al. 2006; U.S. GAO 2006.
8. Urrea 2004: 120–29. Also see Keim et al. 2006; McConahay 2007.
9. Ellingwood 2004: 55.
10. Office of Public Affairs 1998.
11. "Looking for Answers" 1998.
12. "Death in the Desert" 1998.
13. "Hard Line on Human Coyotes" 1998.
14. Associated Press 1998b. The corpse of one of the smugglers—a sixteen-year-old male— was discovered on a different day about five miles away from the group of seven. Authorities determined that he was working with the smuggler found dead among the group of seven that included Julio César Gallegos. All together, authorities found ten bodies in the same general area—one on July 3, another on August 12, seven on August 13, and one more on August 19. The Border Patrol surmised that they were all part of the same group of crossers. See Associated Press 1998a; Henry 1998.
15. The approach this book employs is, in part, inspired by the well-known work of Angus Wright (2005), *The Death of Ramón González: The Modern Agricultural Dilemma*. Wright's classic book tells the story of one Mexican farm worker and his death from pesticide poi-

229

soning as a way of explicating a larger cycle of farming-related suffering brought about by a complex array of factors and processes associated with industrial agriculture, modern human-environment relations, and a corporate-dominated world economy.

16. Regarding places, see Curry 1996; Massey 1993 and 2005; Price 2004.

TWO **THE DESERT**

1. *CCBRES Bulletin*, January 2005 and May–June 2006.
2. DeBuys 1996.
3. Hundley 1975: 17–19; see also Forbes 1965.
4. Henricks 1971; Laflin 1995; and Landis 2000: 40.
5. See Limerick 1989.
6. Street 2004a: 475.
7. Hendricks 1971: 14.
8. Laflin 1995, Hundley 1975: 21.
9. Street 2004a: 475.
10. Wright 1999: 69.
11. See Bokovoy 1999.
12. Wright 1999: 86.
13. Wright 1999: 153–54.
14. Wright 1999: 395.
15. Wright 1999: 68–69.
16. Wright 1999: 380.
17. Wright 1999: 414–15.
18. See McWilliams 1968: 89–90; Takaki 1993: 169.
19. Almaguer 1994: 7–8.
20. Almaguer 1994: 8; see also Pitt 1966.
21. Almaguer 1994: 26–28 and Takaki 1993: 178. Also see Forbes 1965; Pitt 1966.
22. Stannard 1992: 21–24, 134–42.
23. Stannard 1992: 146; see also pp. 142–45, as well as Heizer and Almquist 1971.
24. Takaki 1993: 178. See also Heizer and Almquist 1971; Menchaca 1995; Takaki 1993.
25. Takaki 1993: 182.
26. Takaki 1993: 184–87; see also Almaguer 1994: 29–32 and 65–73, Vélez-Ibáñez 1997 ; and McWilliams 1968: 132.
27. Bokovoy 1999; Street 2004: 491–492.
28. See Taylor 1928; Iwata 1992; Leonard 1992.
29. See Bokovoy 1999; Ferguson 1947; Guerin-Gonzales 1994: 19–22; Ichioka 1988; Iwata 1992; Ngai 2004: 40–41; Walker 2004: 81
30. Cornelius 1978: 14; see also Guerin-Gonzales 1994, chapter 2; Zolberg 2006: 240–41.
31. Taylor 1928.
32. McWilliams 1968: 189–90.
33. Quoted in Romo 1983: 114–15. As cited, quotation taken from U.S. Department of Labor, Bureau of Labor Statistics, "Mexican Labor in the Imperial Valley of California," *Monthly Labor Review* 28 (March 1929): 62.

34. Steinbeck 1988: 53–54. See also Reisler 1976: 181.
35. Quoted in Sánchez 1993: 96. According to Sánchez's endnote, quotation taken from U.S. Congress, House, Committee on Immigration and Naturalization, *Hearings on Temporary Admission of Illiterate Mexican Laborers*, 69th Congress, 1st session, 1926, 191, and *Hearings on Seasonal Agricultural Laborers from Mexico*, 46.
36. California and a number of other states in the Southwest and West had laws against miscegenation, restrictions that were widespread throughout much of the United States. The states with such bans included Arizona, Nevada, and Oregon. California's ban on marriage and cohabitation between a "Caucasian" and a "Negro, mulatto, or Mongolian" ("Malay" was added to the list in 1945) lasted from 1880 until 1948. Nevada's prohibitions stayed in place until 1959, Utah's until 1963, Texas's until 1970. See Orenstein 2005; Pascoe 1991 and 1996.
37. Quoted in Reisler 1976: 180.
38. Quoted in McWilliams 1968: 190.
39. Hundley 1975: 27.
40. Weber 1972.
41. Walker 2004: 43–44.
42. Rorty 1935. See also McWilliams 1939; Walker 2004.
43. Rorty 1935: 575.
44. See Mitchell 1996: 105–6.
45. Harris 1956–58: 31.
46. See Gamio 1930.
47. Both quotes in Taylor 1928: 40.
48. Steinbeck 1988: 23.
49. The Mexican Revolution began in 1910. It started as a rebellion against the government of Porfirio Díaz, which many in Mexico saw as overly beholden to the interests of large landowners, foreign capitalists, and the United States government. The war involved many different political and armed groups. Although the war officially ended in 1917, associated violence continued for a number of years thereafter. See Gilly 2005.
50. See Gordon 2001; Sandos 1992.
51. Miller 2005: 172–74.
52. Quoted in Reisler 1976: 242.
53. Regarding labor organizing and repression in the Imperial Valley in the early 1900s, see DeWitt 1980; Dinwoodie 1977; González 1996; McWilliams 1939; Miller 2005; Rorty 1935; Street 2004a and b; Weber 1972; Wollenberg 1969.
54. McWilliams 1949: 303.
55. Steinbeck 1988: 37.
56. According to Kitty Calavita (1992: 1–2), "What came to be called the Bracero Program was in fact a series of programs initiated by administrative fiat, subsequently endorsed by Congress, and kept alive by executive agreement whenever foreign relations or domestic politics threatened their demise."
57. London and Anderson 1970: 118–21.
58. See London and Anderson 1970: 50–52.
59. Bardacke 2006.

60. Miller 2005: 205.
61. Street 1980: 46.
62. See Street 2004b: 271 and 274.
63. Street 1980; Pawel 2006; Bardacke 2006. On April 23, 1979, a local municipal court judge, one married to a strikebreaker, dismissed murder charges against three foremen arrested for the murder on the grounds that the bullet that actually killed him could not be found. The foreman actually admitted shooting at Contreras. Nonetheless, no other charges were brought against them.
64. Hundley 1975: 22; see also Martínez Zepada et al. 1991.
65. Duncan 1994. See also Monroy 1999: 73; Herzog 1990: 92–93.
66. See Delgado 2004; Lee 2003.
67. Duncan 1994; Lucero 2003.
68. For information on the history and development of *ejidos*, see Wright 2005.
69. Lucero 2003: 102–105.
70. Arreola and Curtis 1993: 20–21; Duncan 1994; Schantz 2001: 558–559.
71. Herzog 1990: 97–98; and Ruiz 2000: Chapter 3.
72. Schantz 2001: 549–51, 554.
73. Lucero 2003: 104–6.
74. *CCBRES Bulletin*, May/June 2006.
75. Lucero 2003 108–12.
76. See, for example, Germani 1991.
77. Buffington 1994: 28–31.
78. Border-crossing cards are visas issued to Mexican nationals who meet certain eligibility requirements. The cards allow their holders to cross into the United States and conduct business (not including paid work) or engage in recreational activities for up to 72 hours. BCC holders are generally required to stay within 25 miles of the U.S.-Mexico boundary, although in some areas of the border region they are allowed to go further north. In southern Arizona, for example, BCC holders are allowed to go as far as Tucson, about 65 miles north of the boundary.

    U.S. nationals do not need a visa or passport to enter Mexico via its northern boundary. Only if one wants to stay in Mexico for more than 72 hours, or go beyond the border zone (generally about 20 miles south of the international boundary, although it extends much further south in the case of Baja California) does one need to obtain a visa, which is easily obtainable within Mexican territory.
79. See Chey 1998; Huffaker 2006; Marosi 2004b.
80. Marosi 2004b. The attitudes of Americans of Mexican descent toward migrants from Mexico and beyond are complex, and contingent on a variety of factors, a key one being how many generations they have been in the United States. One should not assume Mexican-Americans as a whole to be any less "American" than other ethnic group in the United States simply because the United States shares a boundary with Mexico. Indeed, Mexican-Americans, while opposing specific immigration and boundary-related initiatives in greater numbers than the general population—due to their discriminatory focus on people of Mexican descent—have historically supported immigration and boundary enforcement at levels similar to those of the white population. In this regard, Mexican-Americans are just as "American" as any other

national origin group in the United States. Like all people, Mexican-Americans have multiple identities; in their particular case, while many often strongly distinguish themselves from non-Mexican-origin Americans and embrace their Mexican heritage, many also often harbor strong anti-Mexican sentiment. This is hardly a surprising outcome given that people of Mexican descent in the United States are also—to varying degrees—"American" and thus have been similarly socialized to think in terms of "us" and "them," "our" territory and "theirs." See Binder et al. 1997; Gutiérrez 1995; Vila 2000; Waldinger 2007.

81. See Burawoy 1976; Petras 1980.
82. Notimex 1998.
83. Furillo 2001.
84. Berestein and Lindquist 2007.
85. See Marosi 2004a.
86. For photographs of water-engineering projects in the Valley during the first half of the 20th century, see Livernois 1982.
87. Quotes from Hundley 1975: 33–34.
88. Hundley 1975: 28.
89. Hundley 2001: 208–13.
90. Huffaker 2006.
91. deBuys 1996: 116.
92. Perry 2006.
93. Regarding the importance and power of the Colorado River in shaping the area over millennia, modern-day attempts to tame it, and ways in which the river has fought back, see Forbes 1965; Hundley 1975 and 2001; Reisner 1993; Worster 1985. Thanks to Frank Bardacke for making me appreciate the significance of this matter.
94. Laflin 1995; Landis 2000; Streitfeld 2007.
95. Regarding the historical misuse of water in the Imperial Valley, see McWilliams 1949.
96. See, for example, Kelly 2007.
97. Obsatz 2003; see also Ellingwood 2004.
98. Ellingwood 2004: 203.
99. Taylor 1928: 27–28.
100. Berestein 2006; also see Ellingwood 2004 and LeDuff 2004.
101. See letter from Inspector in Charge, Calexico, CA to Supervising Inspector, Immigration Service, El Paso, TX, Jan. 11, 1918, NARA file 60-A-600. Copy of letter on file with author.
102. "The Border Patrol" 1927.
103. Reeves 1981: 126.
104. NARA file 4302/44.
105. Guerin-Gonzales 1994: 73–74.
106. See, for example, the 1951 photo at http://www.latinamericanstudies.org/deportation.htm. The caption reads: "A group of illegal Mexican workers, involved in a farm labor strike in Imperial Valley, CA., board a Flying Tiger airliner at El Centro, June 1, 1951, to be deported to their homes in Guadalajara, Mexico."
107. "Wetbacks Swarm In" 1951: 33 and 35.
108. Quotes taken from Eckels 1954: 28 and 30. Cited in García 1980: 157.

THREE **THE BORDER**

1. See, for example, Truett 2006.
2. That said, in terms of the making of the U.S.-Mexico boundary as a line of control, the process has long been very much a U.S.-dominated one. Of course, this reflects the highly unequal relations between the United States and Mexico, and the associated fact that the former, as the more powerful party, has a far greater interest in regulating migration across the boundary than does the latter.
3. Vázquez and Meyer 1985: 13–15 and Martínez 1995: 8–10.
4. Vázquez and Meyer 1985: 16 and Griswold del Castillo 1990: 8–11.
5. Williams 1981: 156.
6. See Horsman 1981; Ross 1998; Stephanson 1995.
7. Acuña 1988: 6.
8. Vázquez and Meyer 1985: 21. For a thorough analysis of "manifest destiny" as an ideology, see Weinberg 1963.
9. See, for example, Takaki 1993: 173.
10. Martínez 1995: 11–14. See Perea 2003 re: the role of slavery in U.S. efforts to acquire Texas.
11. For an account of the war, see Williams 1981, chapter 8.
12. For the full text of the treaty, see Martínez 1996 or Griswold del Castillo 1990.
13. See maps, Appendices B and C.
14. Reséndez 2006: 93.
15. See Reséndez 2006.
16. Quoted in Takaki 1993: 172.
17. Martínez 1995: 17–21, 43; and Griswold del Castillo 1990: 55–61.
18. A filibuster is a term applied to individuals from the United States who sought to steal territory from Mexico, or overthrow foreign governments—in Central America, for example—for various reasons, but most typically economic gain.
19. Martínez 1995: 44–46 and 51. Porfirio Díaz ruled Mexico in 1876, and 1877–1880; 1884–1911. For an analysis of his reign, see Ross 1998, chapter 4. See also Gonzalez 2006.
20. See Dunn 1996; Johnson 2003.
21. Johnson 2003: 12.
22. See Perea 2003.
23. See Dunn 1996; Johnson 2003.
24. Martínez 1995.
25. Dunn 1996; Martínez 1995. See also Nadelmann 1993: 69–76.
26. See Dunn 1996: 10–11.
27. Dowty 1987; Harris 2002; Torpey 2000.
28. Torpey 2000: 159. The citation for the study John Torpey references is: Werner Bertelsmann, *Das Passwesen: eine völkerrechtliche Studie*, Strassburg: J. H. Ed. Heitz, 1914.
29. The one exception is the Alien Enemies Act of 1798. While the Alien Friends Act of 1798 expired after only two years, the Alien Enemies remains in force—in modified form—through today. It empowers the president to detain, relocate, or deport "enemy aliens" during a time of war.

30. See Haney López 1996; Lee 2003; Nevins 2002; Ngai 2004.
31. The newly created Immigration Service took over immigration and boundary enforcement functions in the 1890s.
32. See Perkins 1978; Taylor H. 1994.
33. Grebler 1966: 19.
34. Grebler 1966: 19.
35. Brown 1991: 66.
36. Logan 1969: 72.
37. Letter from Inspector in Charge, Tia Juana, California, to Supervising Inspector, Immigration Service, El Paso, Texas, January 9, 1918. Copy of letter on file with author.
38. NARA file 54261/276.
39. Sánchez 1993: 54–56.
40. Legal immigration declined from 90,000 in 1924 to 32,378 the year following the implementation of the 1924 act (Sánchez 1993: 57). According to http://www.measuringworth.com/ppowerus, the $18 in fees in 1924 is the equivalent of approximately $212 in 2006 dollars.
41. Galarza 1964: 61.
42. Sánchez 1993: 56–59.
43. Coppock 1968: 2–4, and U.S. INS 1991: 9–11. See also NARA file 54261/267.
44. Coppock 1968: 4–6 and U.S. INS 1991: 23.
45. See Wixon 1934 for a description by an INS official of the nature of the Border Patrol and the challenges faced by the agency in the early 1930s.
46. Coppock 1968: 9–10, U.S. INS 1991: 23, Dunn 1996: 12, and Wixon 1934: 6.
47. Dunn 1996: 13, and Coppock 1968: 11–12.
48. See Wixon 1934.
49. Wilmoth 1934: 6–7, 9.
50. See Calavita 1994: 60.
51. Galarza 1964: 61.
52. Calavita 1994: 61.
53. McWilliams 1968: 190–92. See also Escobar 1999.
54. Quoted in Wollenberg 1969: 57.
55. Takaki 1993: 333.
56. Balderrama and Rodríguez 1995: 52–53.
57. Cornelius 1978.
58. Cornelius 1978: 16–17, and Cockcroft 1986: 61.
59. See Grebler 1966: 32.
60. Calavita 1992: 24–25.
61. Calavita 1992: 28.
62. Calavita 1992: 47–50.
63. Quoted in Dunn 1996: 14. See also García 1980.
64. Calavita 1992: 50–56.
65. See García 1980.
66. Dunn 1996: 17–18. See also Acuña 1988: 374–75.

67. Dunn 1996: 18; Walters 1990: 10; Fernández and Pedroza 1982; Cardenas 1979: 83; and Lewis 1979: 137–41.
68. Chapman assumed the position of INS commissioner in December 1973.
69. Acuña 1996: 115.
70. Ostrow 1974.
71. Cockcroft 1986: 39.
72. Quoted in Rico 1992: 261.
73. Acuña 1988: 374.
74. *New York Times* 1974.
75. Chapman 1976: 190, emphasis in the original.
76. See Calavita 1994; Diamond 1996; Dunn 1996; Nevins 2002.
77. Quote from Gutiérrez 1995: 200; see also Dunn 1996: 36.
78. The Mariel boatlift took place between April 20 and September 26, 1980. See Zucker and Zucker 1996.
79. Dunn 1996: 36–37.
80. Dunn 1996: 36–41.
81. Dunn 1996: 41–42.
82. Dunn 1996: 42–45.
83. Dunn 1996: 103–05. See also Andreas 2000.
84. Regarding the characterization of the boundary buildup as "militarization," see Dunn 1996.
85. Davis 1995; Nevins 2002.
86. Schrag 1998.
87. Schrag 1998; Walker 1995 and 1996.
88. See Andreas 2000; Calavita 1994.
89. See Diamond 1996; Conniff 1993; and Barnes 1994.
90. Milton 1993; Popkin and Friedman 1993; Zucker and Zucker 1996.
91. Kwong 1997; McDonald 1997; Morganthau 1993; Rotella 1998; Thomas 1993; Zucker and Zucker 1996.
    Prior to the *Golden Venture* incident, in mid-May, U.S. authorities discovered a shipload of 198 smuggled Chinese immigrants off the coast of San Diego. Just two weeks prior, Mexican authorities had apprehended a shipload of 306 Chinese immigrants—all of whom reportedly intended to go to the United States—off the coast of Ensenada, south of Tijuana. See Lau 1993 and Gross 1993.
92. Barnes 1994; Conniff 1993; King and Foote 1993; Murr 1993; Walczak 1994.
93. In terms of the making of the U.S-Mexico boundary, its apparatus of control, exclusion and inclusion, and the related social categories, Mexico has also played a significant role. In the early 1960s, for instance, the Mexican government, as part of the *Programa Nacional Fronterizo* (PRONAF), or National Border Program, constructed a variety of cultural and educational centers in the border region. The country's Secretary of Public Education targeted the northern border region for increased dissemination of books on Mexico and for the development of school programs aimed at strengthening national identity, which many Mexican elites felt was under threat due to excessive U.S. influence. In the late 1960s and early 1970s, Mexican officials prevented U.S. "hippies" and men with long hair from enter-

ing Tijuana at various times for fear that hippies were influencing Mexican nationals in terms of dress and anti-work attitudes. And, since the 1980s, Mexican officials have cooperated in various ways with their U.S. counterparts to limit unauthorized migration to the United States, and to regulate the area around the boundary (see Nevins 2002). However, the United States is by far the dominant party in this story of boundary-making given the profound inequality in terms of social power that characterizes the binational relationship.

94. Harris 1956–1958: 31. For various first-person accounts of Border Patrols agents working in the El Centro Sector (which covers the Imperial Valley) through the mid-1970s, see Odens 1981.

95. Ngai 2004: 18.

96. See Fairchild 2003.

97. Romo 2005: 228–229, 237. See also Johnson 2004.

98. Quoted in Fairchild 2003: 150. Source as cited: Commissioner General of Immigration, *Annual Report*, 1906: 69.

99. Fairchild 2003: 18 and 210.

100. Romo 2005: 229.

101. Romo 2005: 235.

102. See Fairchild 2003; Romo 2005; Stern 2005. It is unclear what the negative effects on spraying Zyklon B on the clothing of migrant boundary crossers had on their health, but according to David Romo, anecdotal evidence suggests that it contributed to many deaths, birth defects, and cases of cancer. See also Spike 2007.

103. See Stern 2005.

104. Bacon 2005.

105. See Chang 2000; Mattingly 2004; Nevins 2002; Ngai 2004; Zolberg 2006.

106. Quoted in Davis 2007.

107. See Davis 2007; Feagin 1997; and Perea 1997.

108. Johnson 2004; Kanstroom 2007; Luibheid 2005.

109. See Fernandes 2006; Johnson 2004; Meeropol 2005; Nguyen 2005.

110. U.S. Congress 1994: 36.

111. See Sparke 2006.

112. Marosi 2004b.

113. Henry 1998: A11–A12; Mozingo 1998.

114. Regarding the insignificant impact enforcement has had on the flow of illicit drugs across the boundary, see Andreas 2000.

115. Cornelius 2006 and 2007; Fuentes et al. 2007. For those trying to get to the United States from elsewhere, but via Mexico, it is certainly far tougher to reach their destination given the difficulties non-Mexican nationals have in entering and traversing Mexican territory. No doubt, the percentage of such migrants who eventually succeed in reaching the United States is lower than that of Mexican migrants. See Aizenman 2006; Flynn 2002; Thompson 2006.

116. See Marosi 2007; McKinley 2007; Riley 2007.

117. See, for example, Marosi 2004b.

118. See Allegro 2006; Coleman 2007; Cook 2003; Dow 2004, Fernandes 2006; Gaouette and Bustillo 2007; Heyman 1999a and 1999b; Hing 2006; Kanstroom 2007; Kateel and Sha-

hani, forthcoming; Meeropol 2005; Nevins 2005a; Nguyen 2005; Rosas 2007; and Silko 2003.

119. See, for example, Associated Press 2007.
120. Fix and Zimmerman 1999.
121. See, for example, Bernstein 2004 and 2005; Cooper 2007a; Danticat 2007.
122. See, for example, Alvarez 2006.
123. Brofenbrenner 2000. See also Bachelet 2007; De Genova 2005.
124. Regarding the growing significance of the citizen-noncitizen divide, see Kateel and Shahani, forthcoming.

FOUR **JUCHIPILA, MEXUSA**

1. See Levitt 2001; Wise 2006;
2. See http://www.juchipila.com for an online directory of many of the Juchipilans living in the United States.
3. In 2000, the population of the *municipio* was 12,662—9,414 of whom lived in Juchipila proper, with the residing in the eighteen other localities of the municipio. See López Robles 2000.
4. Lindstrom 1995; López Robles 2000.
5. Lindstrom 1995; López Robles 2000.
6. See Azuela 1963, biographical note about author.
7. Azuela 1963: 141.
8. Lindstrom 1995: 50; López Robles 2000: 57.
9. Lindstrom 1995: 90.
10. Lindstrom 1995: 88.
11. See López Robles 2000: 59–60; McAllen 1999; Thompson 2001.
12. Lindstrom 1995: 88–89.
13. Padilla 2000: 369.
14. Hernandez Jáuregui 2004.
15. Quoted in *Shadow of Hope* 2004. The English translation contained here differs slightly from the one contained on the online transcript. The author made the changes based on hearing the actual words of the mayor.
16. See González and Fernandez 2002.
17. Massey et al. 2002: 31.
18. The Southern Pacific Railroad and the Santa Fe Railroad, for example, had Mexican subsidiaries. Meanwhile U.S. capitalists had controlling interests in what were nominally Mexican railroad companies. Oilman Henry Clay Pierce, for instance, was a majority owner of the Mexican Central Railroad.
19. Cornelius 1978; Massey et al. 2002: 27–30; Monroy 1999: 89–93. See also González and Fernandez 2002; Guerin-Gonzales 1994; Romo 1983, Chapter 3.
20. Balderrama and Rodríguez 1995: 6–7.
21. Grebler 1966: 20–21, and Cornelius 1978: 14–15. See also Massey et al. 2002.
22. Grebler 1966: 21, and Cornelius 1978: 15.
23. Balderrama and Rodríguez 1995: 7; Monroy 1999: 93–94.

24. Cross and Sandos 1982: 13.
25. Calavita 1992; Cornelius 1978; Cockcroft 1986; Massey et al. 2002.
26. Cornelius 1978: 17–18; see also Massey et al. 2002: 41. Regarding the abusive and exploitative nature of the Bracero Program, see González 2006.
27. Massey et al. 2002: 42, 47–51.
28. Cañas, Coronado, and Gilmer 2006. According to the publication, the "backbone" of the bilateral trade relationship is comprised of temporary imports that are re-exported. These temporary imports are parts which are used in assembling products sent to the United States. Industrial products make up 82 percent of Mexico's exports to the United States, and 91 percent of U.S. exports to Mexico. Approximately half of U.S.–Mexico trade is considered intra-industry trade, largely due to these temporary imports.
29. Polaski 2003: 17–19.
30. Massey et al. 2002. See also Nevins 2007.
31. Batalova 2006: 1 and 5.
32. Associated Press 2006; Williams 2006.
33. See McAllen 1999.
34. Jones 1995, Chapter 2.
35. Delgado Wise and Moctezuma Longoria 1993.
36. Monroy 1999: 80.
37. Jones 1995: 33.
38. Cross and Sandos 1982: 6–7; Jones 1995: 33.
39. Azuela 1963: 144–145.
40. The 1917 Mexican Constitution had a number of articles which weakened the Church's hand in domestic affairs. Among other things, the constitution nationalized all the Church's real estate held by third parties such as schools and hospitals, while prohibiting clergy from taking part in politics and voting and banning the publication of religious journals that touched upon political matters. While the revolutionary government did not strongly enforce the laws for a number of years, tensions erupted in 1926 when Plutarco Elías Calles, president of Mexico from 1924 to 1928, tried to enforce and strengthen some the anticlerical aspects of the revolutionary constitution.
41. Cross and Sandos 1982: 8–9; Monroy 1999: 85–87.
42. Gilly 2005: 386 (note 5).
43. Cross and Sandos 1982: 11–12; Jones 1995: 33. See also Wright 2005.
44. Esparza 2004; López Robles 2004.
45. Lindstrom 1995: 74–77, 102 and 131.
46. Acuña 1984: 4; Flamming 2005: 20; Poole and Ball 2002: 8–11.
47. Acuña 1984: 4; Deverell 2004: 96-97; Poole and Ball 2002: 13.
48. Griswold del Castillo 1979; Acuña 1988.
49. Molina 2006: 4 and 7.
50. Deverell 2004: 15. See also Griswold del Castillo 1979.
51. Acuña 1988; Bokovoy 1999; Griswold del Castillo 1979: 41–51; Pitt 1998.
52. See Acuña 1988; Dunn 1996; Pitt 199; Poole and Ball 2002.
53. Acuña 1998: 127–28.
54. Acuña 1984: 7–8.

55. Romo 1983: 60 and 114.

56. Quoted in Deverell 2004: 4.

57. Quoted in Romo 1983: 114. As cited, the original source of the quote is Robert N. McLean, "Mexican Workers in the United States," in *National Conference of Social Work, Proceedings* (Chicago, 1929), 537.

58. Quoted in McWilliams 1968: 190.

59. Quoted in Monroy 1999: 110.

60. See Balderrama and Rodríguez 1995: 16; Monroy 1999: 110.

61. Romo 1983: 60.

62. Balderrama and Rodríguez 1995: 55, 57–58.

63. Sánchez 1993: 209–10.

64. Molina 2006: 136, 140–41.

65. Acuña 1996: 112.

66. Monroy 1999: 27–29.

67. For an in-depth study of how discrimination against, and segregation of, Latinos function in one Southern California community, Santa Paula, see Menchaca 1995.

68. The zoot suit was not only a clothing style among many working class, African American and Latino youth, but also a sign of opposition to a highly racialized, economic order, and often to the military draft, which many evaded during World War II. See Kelley 1997.

69. Acuña 1988: 254–59; Escobar 1999. See also McWilliams 1968.

70. The change was most likely due to many factors, including efforts by members of racially subordinated groups and their allies to challenge racist ideology and practice and a discrediting of overtly racist thinking brought about the revulsion many felt toward Nazi Germany.

71. See Acuña 1988: 258.

72. Normark 1999.

73. See García 1980, chapter 7.

74. See Escobar 1999.

75. Varsanyi 2005: 132, note 9.

76. Cooper 2007b.

77. Massey and Denton 1994.

78. Logan et al. 2001.

79. Flamming 2005: 204–5.

80. Flamming 2005: 20; Poole and Ball 2002.

81. Flamming 2005: 2.

82. Banks 2006.

83. See Flamming 2005; Sides 2003. See also Hamilton 1987.

84. See Iwata 1992.

85. See Sides 2003: 110.

86. Banks 2005; Sides 2003: 101.

87. See Banks 2005; Bonacich and Goodman 1972. For a broad, somewhat anecdotal account of Inglewood's history, see Waddingham 1994.

88. For additional information regarding Inglewood's history as a "sundown town," see http://www.uvm.edu/~jloewen/sundowntownsshow.php?id=21.

89. For an interesting discussion of contemporary Inglewood, see Aubry Kaplan 2005. See also Faussett 2002.
90. See Alarcón 2002; Fox 2006; Root 2006; Zabin and Escala 2002.
91. Reeves 1981: 116.
92. Acuña 1984: 6.
93. Acuña 1984: 13–14; see also Romo 1983: 65–67, 78–80, 144. Regarding the removal of Japanese Americans from Boyle Heights, see Fleming 1998; Sánchez 2002
94. Quoted in Sanchez 2004: 633. As cited in Sanchez 2004, the quotation are taken from, respectively: "Boyle Heights: A Sociological Fishbowl," *Fortnight*, October 20, 1954: 2023; and Ralph Friedman, "U.N. in Microcosm: Boyle Heights: An Example of Democratic Progress," *Frontier: The Voice of the New West*, March 1955: 12.
95. Sánchez 2004: 634. For a photographic history of Boyle Heights, see Japanese American National Museum 2005.
96. See Sánchez 2002: 9–10.
97. Acuña 1984: 14; Pardo 1998: 71.
98. Pardo 1998: 72.
99. Sánchez 2002: 3.
100. Acuña 1988: 173–74. See also Sánchez 2004.
101. Loewen 2005: 75. For an overview of the history of racially-motivated housing restrictions and the construction of "white walls" in and around Los Angeles, see Davis 1990: 159–169.
102. Reeves 1981: 143.
103. Wild 2002.
104. Quoted in Varzally 2003: 16. Quote taken from the Roosevelt High student newspaper: "Roosevelt—A Melting Pot," *Rough Rider*, October 3, 1940.
105. Fleming 1998.
106. Reeves 1981. Regarding the Chicano movement and the walkouts, see Haney López 2003. See Pulido 2006 regarding the Chicano movement in Los Angeles.
107. Sánchez 2002.
108. Acuña 1984: 184.
109. Haney López 2003: 16.
110. Just southeast of downtown Los Angeles, Vernon was incorporated in 1905 as a haven for so-called sporting activities (boxing, gambling, and drinking), eventually evolving in the 1920s into an "exclusively industrial" city—as is today officially proclaimed by the city's motto. Vernon is one of about a half-dozen, local "phantom cities", in the words of historian Mike Davis, industrial districts in and around Los Angeles that have been incorporated as cities to monopolize control of land and the tax base. Most of the city's workers receive wages so low that 96 percent of them qualify for public housing assistance. Vernon is the greater Los Angeles area's biggest source of pollution. Its two biggest growth industries are "ethnic-food" processing and toxic waste disposal. In 2006, Vernon had an official residential population of only 91 people, most of whom were city employees or their family members, and a heavy concentration of manufacturing plants, which, together, draw into the city 44,000 workers daily. See Davis 2002: 191-196; Bercerra, Connell, and Lopez 2006.
111. Regarding the importance of unauthorized Latino workers in the Los Angeles economy, see Marcelli 1999.

FIVE **BEYOND THE BOUNDARY**

1. Henry 1998: A11.
2. Mozingo 1998: B5.
3. See print editions of Henry 1998; Mozingo 1998.
4. See Henry 1998; "Looking for Answers" 1998; Mozingo 1998. When I interviewed Don Florentino at his home in Juchipila, Zacatecas, on January 16, 2002, he was less certain about the matter of blame. "I don't blame anyone. It has passed," he said. "Maybe the *coyotes* are to blame for leaving him there. It's not worth the trouble trying to blame anyone." Don Florentino, who passed away in 2004, had not heard at that point that the smugglers had died along with his son.
5. See Nevins 2005b, note 70 for examples of such.
6. See Doty 2007.
7. No one—at least on the basis of the press reports on the funeral—said anything that would suggest that the INS and its policing of the border had anything to do with the death.
8. Louie Gilot, "Boy Pulls Mother's Body Across NM Desert" *El Paso Times*, August 1, 2006.
9. See http://minutemanhq.com/b2/index.php/national/2006/08/.
10. See the text of the Border Protection, Antiterrorism, and Illegal Immigration Control Act of 2005, H.R. 4437 at http://www.govtrack.us/congress/billtext.xpd?bill=h109-4437.
11. Quoted in Scully 2006.
12. See Krauthammer 2007.
13. Quoted in Cooper 2006.
14. Both quotes from Calavita 1992: 50. Original source: United States Congress, *Congressional Record: Proceedings and Debates of the 83rd Congress Second Session*, Volume 100, Part 2, Washington, D.C.: United States Government Printing Office, 1954: 2558 and 2560.
15. See Bustillo 2006; Maril 2004
16. See, for example, Agence France Press 2007; Marosi 2006; Reuters 2006a; Weissert 2006; Welch 2006.
17. Leiken and Brooke 2006.
18. See, for example, Rumbaut and Ewing 2007; Sampson, Morenoff, and Raudenbush 2005.
19. Mueller 2006.
20. Transactional Records Action Clearinghouse 2007.
21. See Nevins 2002 and 2005b.
22. Quotations from Goodspeed 2003; Martinez 2002. In what is certainly one of the greater ironies in the contemporary U.S.-Mexico borderlands, in 2005 some Border Patrol agents were caught dating, loving, and living with the very "illegals" they are charged with apprehending. See Riccardi 2005.
23. See Rowling 1987; Wolf 1980.
24. SoHo—"South of Houston"—is a neighborhood in Manhattan, New York City.
25. Quotations from Robinovitz 2004.
26. Associated Press 2004.
27. Romero 2004c.
28. Grasmuck and Pessar 1991; Levitt 2001.

29. Fineman 1998.
30. Althaus 2003.
31. Romero 2004a, 2004b.
32. Quoted in Robinovitz 2004.
33. Hall 1992; Gilmore 2002a and 2002b.
34. See, for example, Booker and Minter 2001; Richmond 1994; Sharma 2006.
35. Bremner 2005: 131.
36. Massey, Durand, and Malone, 2002: 49.
37. See Nevins 2002.
38. See Massey, Durand, and Malone, 2002.
39. See Nevins 2002.
40. Chang 2000; Holmes and Greenhouse 2001.
41. Jacobs 1995; Stern 1993 and 1994.
42. I was accompanying the reporter, and overheard the conversation.
43. See Nevins 2003.
44. See Hammer 2006; Harris 2006; Meldrum 2006; Reuters 2006b.
45. Harris 2006.
46. Reuters 2006b.
47. See, for example, Carens 1999 and 2000; Doty 2006; Miller and Hashmi 2001.
48. For arguments in favor of freedom of movement, see Harris 2002; Johnson 2003. Some have restricted their calls for freedom of mobility to movement between the United States and Mexico. See Laufer 2004; Rappleye 2007.
49. For a photo of this scene, see Palafox and Jardine 1999: 21.
50. See Blackhawk 2006.
51. Mayer 2002.
52. See Blackhawk 2006; Drinnon 1997.
53. See Vidal 2004.
54. Massey 1993: 61; see also Massey 2005.
55. See Bacon 2004, 2007a, and 2007b.

INDEX

245

BIOGRAPHICAL NOTES

MIZUE AIZEKI is a documentary photographer. Her work has appeared in a variety of publications including *ColorLines*, *The Progressive*, *L.A. Weekly*, *The Nation*, the *Wall Street Journal*, and *Z Magazine*. She has also exhibited her work in several venues, including the Mission Cultural Center for Latino Arts in San Francisco. She works with organizations in New York City that focus on the impact of detention and deportation, and on worker rights.

JOSEPH NEVINS is the author of *Operation Gatekeeper: The Rise of the "Illegal Alien" and the Making of the U.S.-Mexico Boundary* (Routledge, 2002) and, more recently, *A Not-So-Distant Horror: Mass Violence in East Timor* (Cornell University Press, 2005). His writings have appeared in numerous journalistic publications, including the *Boston Review*, the *Christian Science Monitor*, *CounterPunch*, the *International Herald Tribune*, the *Los Angeles Times*, *The Nation*, and *Z Magazine*. He is an associate professor of geography at Vassar College in Poughkeepsie, New York.